Y0-ADY-368

Hey-O!

Each Bible story in this book has an accompanying animated video, to enhance readers' understanding and provide a full, immersive experience. You can watch the videos separately or as you work your way through the book. Scan the QR code to access animated videos for each of the Hey-O! Stories of the Bible:

HarperCollins Christian Publishing, Inc. and its affiliates are not responsible for maintaining any digital service and access is subject to expiration. No refunds, exchanges, or substitutions. Internet connection required. You will be required to register for StudyGateway.com to access your streaming copy and access will be subject to the site's terms of use: HarperCollinsChristian.com/terms. This code may not be transferred or sold separately. Offer void if obtained through non-authorized channels, including, without limitation, free offer, or freebie directories. Void where prohibited, taxed, or restricted by law.

To:

From:

Date:

Hey-O!
Stories of the Bible

Saddleback Kids

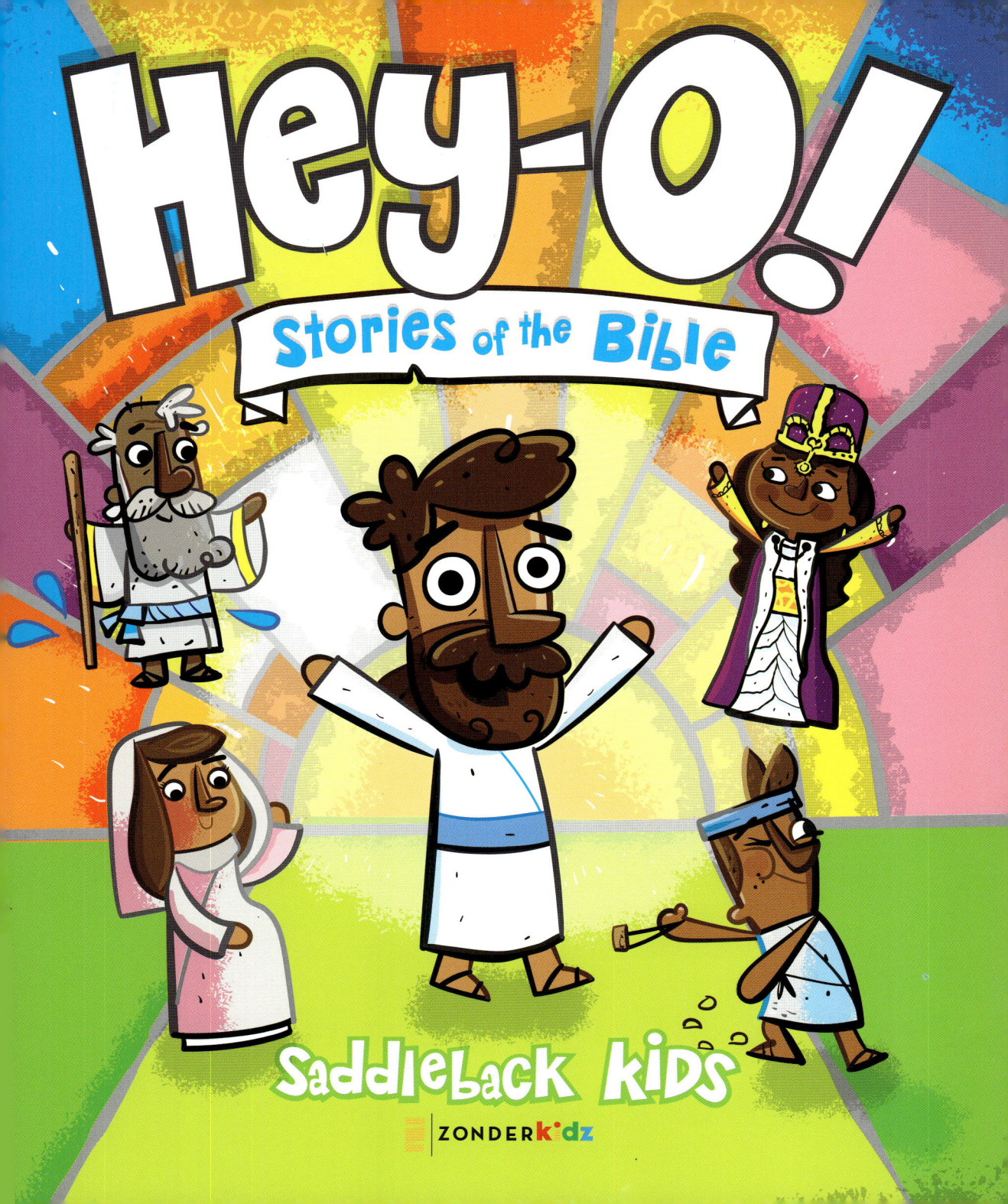

ZonderKidz

ZONDERKIDZ

Hey-O! Stories of the Bible

Copyright © 2024 Saddleback Valley Community Church
Illustrations © 2024 Saddleback Valley Community Church

Published in Grand Rapids, Michigan, by Zonderkidz. Zonderkidz is a registered trademark of HarperCollins Christian Publishing, Inc.

Requests for information should be addressed to customercare@harpercollins.com.

ISBN 978-0-310-15925-4 (hardcover)
ISBN 978-0-310-15931-5 (ebook)

Library of Congress Cataloging-in-Publication Data
ISBN 978-0-310-15925-4

Scripture quotations are taken from the Holy Bible, New International Reader's Version®, NIrV®. Copyright © 1995, 1996, 1998, 2014 by Biblica, Inc.® Used by permission of Zondervan. All rights reserved worldwide. www.Zondervan.com. The "NIrV" and "New International Reader's Version" are trademarks registered in the United States Patent and Trademark Office by Biblica, Inc.®

Any internet addresses (websites, blogs, etc.) and telephone numbers in this book are offered as a resource. They are not intended in any way to be or imply an endorsement by Zondervan, nor does Zondervan vouch for the content of these sites and numbers for the life of this book.

No part of this publication may be reproduced, stored in a retrieval system, or transmitted in any form or by any means—electronic, mechanical, photocopy, recording, or any other—except for brief quotations in printed reviews, without the prior permission of the publisher.

Zondervan titles may be purchased in bulk for educational, business, fundraising, or sales promotional use. For information, please email SpecialMarkets@Zondervan.com.

Written by: Charlotte St. Hilaire and the Saddleback Kids Team
Illustrations: Drew Pocza
Editor: Katherine Easter
Cover design: Patti Evans
Interior design: Mallory Collins

Printed in Malaysia
24 25 26 27 28   VPM   5 4 3 2 1

Note to Readers

Hey-O!

We are so excited for the journey you are about to go on through these stories from the Bible. The Bible is God's special book. It teaches us real stories about people and places from a long time ago. Our hope for this storybook Bible is that it helps you approach the Bible in a fun way, so you can create a lifelong habit of being in the Word of God.

You may be curious why this is called *Hey-O! Stories of the Bible*. It is because these stories started out as animated cartoons we showed the kids in our congregation at Saddleback Church. In these videos, the characters say little phrases like: "Hey-O!" when they first come on screen; or "Huh?" when they are confused. Our kids loved saying these things with them, and it quickly became part of the culture at Saddleback. We hope you'll enjoy free access to these videos through the QR code at the front of this book as you read this Bible.

Our deepest desire is for you to experience Jesus and to know God because of his incredible story. So whether you are a kid, parent, grandparent, aunt, uncle, brother, sister, teacher, or church leader, our prayer is that these stories come to life for you through the power of the Holy Spirit. Remember these are just *some* of the stories in the Bible—there are so many more you can discover in his Word! God's story is still being written, and you can choose to be a part of the incredible kingdom he is building!

—The Saddleback Kids Team

Stories of the Bible

God Makes Everything 10

Adam and Eve Sin 19

Cain and Abel 25

Noah and the Ark 28

God's Promises for Abraham and Sarah 36

Jacob and Esau 44

Joseph's Coat 54

Joseph Forgives His Brothers 62

Baby Moses 71

Moses and the Red Sea 75

The Ten Commandments 86

Joshua and Caleb 88

The Israelites Cross the Jordan .96

The Walls of Jericho. 100

Gideon's 300 Men. 106

Ruth 113

Hannah. 120

God Speaks to Samuel 123

David Chosen to be King 129

David and Goliath 134

Solomon Asks for Wisdom 142

Jehoshaphat 146

Josiah 153

Jonah and the Fish 158

Elijah on Mount Carmel 164

Naaman is Healed 170

The Fiery Furnace 176

Daniel in the Lions' Den 182

Esther's Request to the King . . . 189

Nehemiah Rebuilds the Wall . . . 196

The Story of Christmas 208

Jesus in the Temple 224

John the Baptist 230

Jesus is Baptized 234

Jesus Changes Water into Wine . . .236

Jesus Forgives and Heals a Man Who Could Not Walk 240	Jesus Raises Lazarus from the Dead 311
The Lord's Prayer 246	Jesus Comes to Jerusalem as King 319
The Faith of a Roman Commander. 248	Jesus' Story of the Two Sons . . 324
Jesus' Story of the Farmer 251	The Widow's Offering 328
Jesus Calms the Storm 256	The Last Supper. 330
Jesus Heals a Suffering Woman and Jairus' Daughter. 261	Jesus Washes His Disciples' Feet . . .335
Jesus Feeds the 5,000 270	The Story of Easter 338
Jesus Walks on Water 275	Jesus Appears to Thomas 347
Jesus' Story of the Good Samaritan 280	Jesus Forgives Peter 349
Jesus Visits Mary and Martha . . 286	Jesus Goes to Heaven. 356
Jesus' Story of the Great Banquet 288	The Holy Spirit Comes at Pentecost 359
Jesus' Story of the Lost Sheep. . 293	Peter Heals a Man Who Could Not Walk 364
Jesus' Story of the Lost Son . . . 296	Philip and the Man from Ethiopia 368
The Thankful Man 303	Saul Becomes a Believer 372
Jesus and the Children 306	Paul and Silas in Prison 377
Zacchaeus 308	Not the End 382

The

Old Testament

God Makes Everything

Genesis 1-2

In the beginning, God created the heavens and the earth. The earth didn't have any shape. It was empty and dark, but the Spirit of God was there.

On the first day, God said, "Let there be light." God saw that the light was good. He separated the light from the darkness. God called the light "day" and the darkness "night."

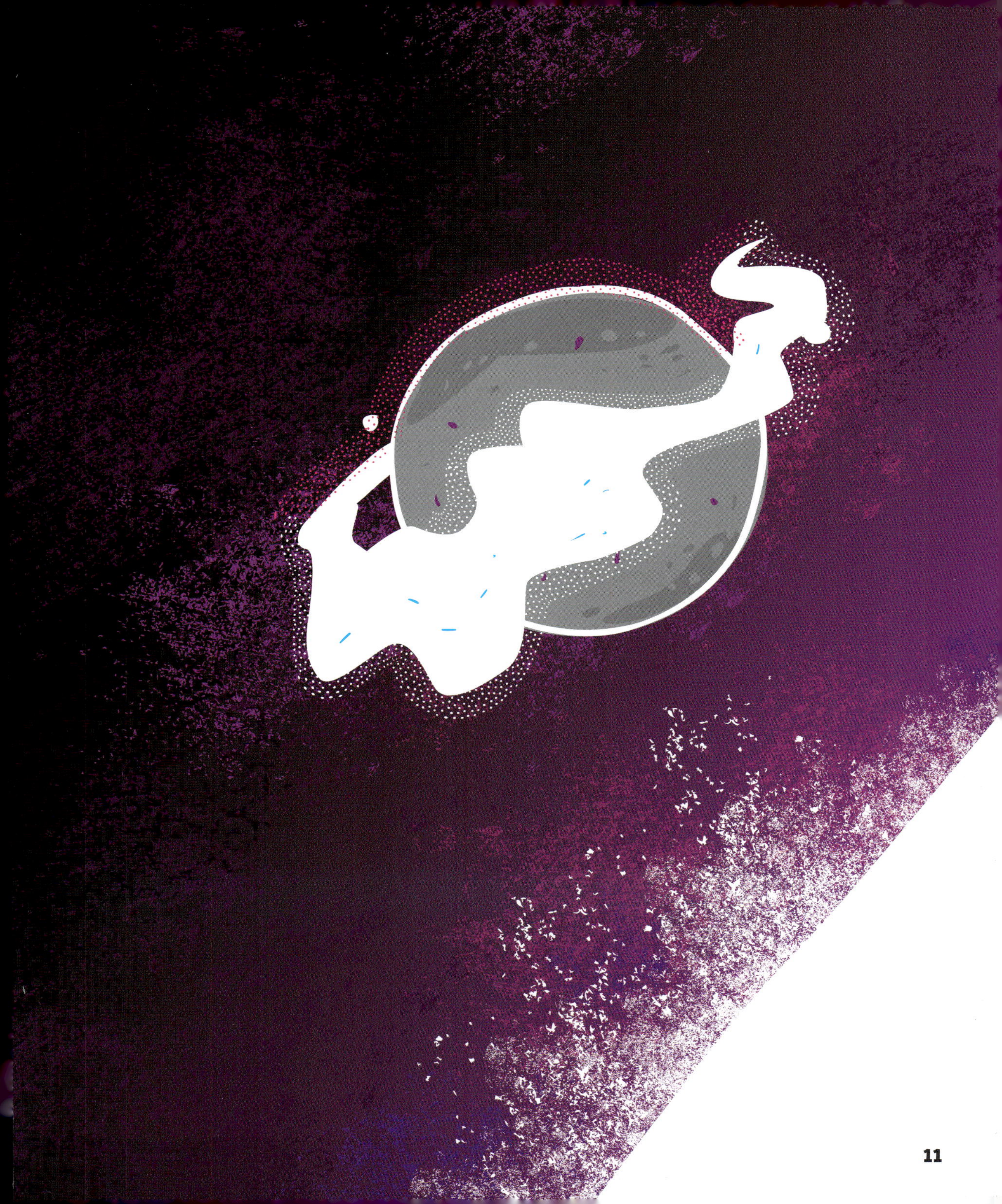

On the second day, God said, "Let there be a huge space between the waters." God called the huge space "sky."

On the third day, God said, "Let the water under the sky be gathered into one place. Let dry ground appear."

God called the dry ground "land" and the waters "seas." Then God said, "Let the land produce plants." And God saw that it was good.

On the fourth day, God said, "Let there be lights in the huge space of the sky. Let them separate the day from the night." God made two great lights—the sun for the day and the moon for the night. He also made the stars. And God saw that it was good.

On the fifth day, God said, "Let the seas be filled with living things. Let birds fly above the earth across the huge space of the sky." God saw that it was good.

On the sixth day, God said, "Let the land produce every kind of living creature." Animals filled the earth.

Then God said, "Let us make human beings so that they are like us."

So God created human beings in his own likeness. He formed man from the dust of the ground. God breathed the breath of life into him. And the man became a living person.

Then he saw that the man needed a helper. So God put man into a deep sleep and took out one of his ribs. Then God made a woman from the rib, brought her to the man, and said, "Have children so that there will be many of you. Fill the earth and bring it under your control. Rule over every living creature."

God saw everything he had made, and it was very good. So, on the seventh day God rested. God blessed the seventh day and made it holy.

Adam and Eve Sin
Genesis 3

This is Adam and this is Eve, who were the first people God made. They lived in the garden of Eden, which was a beautiful place that had everything they needed. There were two trees in the middle of the garden—the tree of life made fruit that would let people live forever, and the other made fruit that gave people the knowledge of good and evil. God told Adam he could eat from any of the trees except the tree of the knowledge of good and evil.

There were lots of animals in the garden, but the serpent was more clever than any of them. One day he asked Eve, "Did God really say, 'You must not eat from any tree in the garden'?"

Eve said they could eat from all of the fruit trees except the tree in the middle of the garden. For God said that if they ate from it, they would die.

"You will not die," the serpent said to the woman. "God knows that when you eat fruit from that tree, you will know things you have never known before. Like God, you will be able to tell the difference between good and evil."

Eve saw that the tree's fruit was ripe and pleasing to look at. She also saw that it would make a person wise. So she took some of the fruit and ate it. Then she gave some to Adam, and he ate it too.

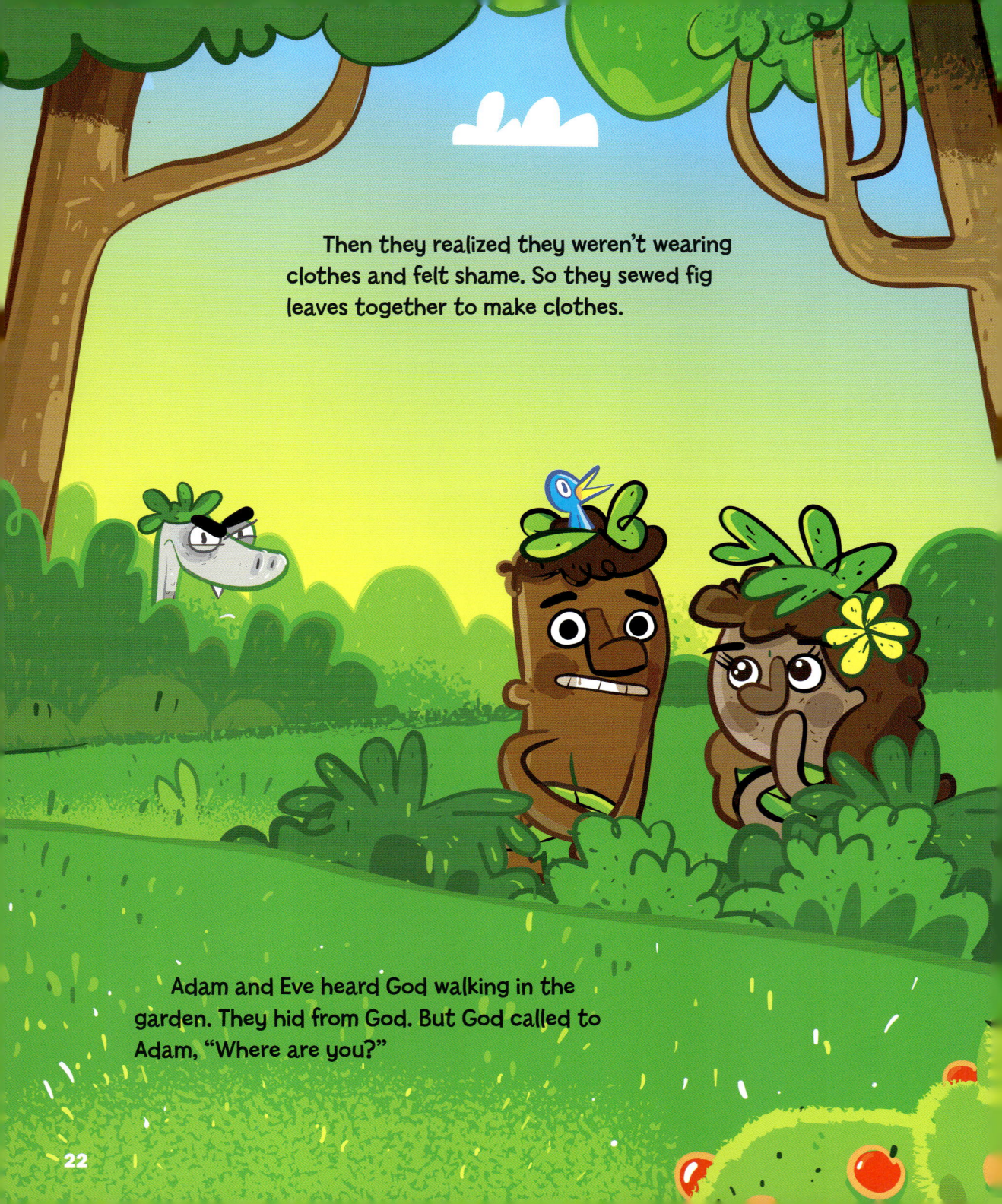

Then they realized they weren't wearing clothes and felt shame. So they sewed fig leaves together to make clothes.

Adam and Eve heard God walking in the garden. They hid from God. But God called to Adam, "Where are you?"

Adam said, "I was afraid, because I was naked. So I hid."

God asked, "Who told you that you were naked? Have you eaten fruit from the tree I commanded you not to eat from?"

Adam blamed Eve and said, "She gave me some fruit from the tree. And I ate it."

Eve said, "The serpent tricked me. That's why I ate the fruit."

Then God punished the serpent by making him crawl on his belly from then on. God said that one day the woman's son would strike his head and he would strike his heel.

Because they did not obey God, he told Eve that she would have great pain when she had children and her husband would rule over her. God told Adam his work would be very difficult. Then God made them clothing from animal skins. God knew that Adam and Eve could no longer live in the garden, so he sent them away and closed it up and placed angels to guard the way to the tree of life.

Cain and Abel

Genesis 4:1-7

Adam and Eve had two sons named Cain and Abel. When Cain and Abel grew up, Cain became a farmer while Abel became a shepherd. When it was time for the harvest, Cain and Abel both brought gifts to God.

Cain gathered some of the things he had grown and gave them to God. God wasn't pleased with Cain and his offering, and this made Cain upset. God asked, "Why are you so angry? Do what is right and then you will be accepted." God warned Cain about sin. God told Cain to be careful to not let sin control him, but instead to take control of sin.

Abel also gave a gift to God. Abel gave God the best part of his firstborn sheep from his flock. God was very pleased with Abel and his offering because he had given the best of what he had.

Noah and the Ark

Genesis 6-9:17

This is Noah. Noah was a good man who walked faithfully with God. But in the time when Noah lived, he was the only one doing the right thing. All the other people on earth were doing mean and harmful things. This made God very sad. So God said he was going to send a flood to earth that would destroy every living thing because he was sorry he ever made them. But God decided to save Noah and his family!

God told Noah to build an ark and fill it with two of every kind of animal. Noah did everything God told him to. Then Noah and his family boarded the ark and waited for the flood to come.

The rain fell hard for forty days and forty nights! Water covered the whole earth, even the highest mountains, but the boat floated on the surface and Noah and his family were safe.

God remembered Noah and all the animals on the ark. So God sent a wind to sweep over the earth.

After five months, the boat came to rest on a mountain.

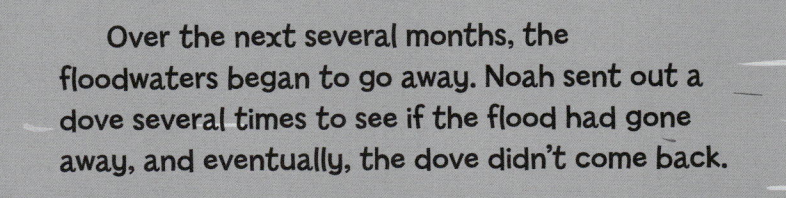

Over the next several months, the floodwaters began to go away. Noah sent out a dove several times to see if the flood had gone away, and eventually, the dove didn't come back.

Noah opened the covering of the ark and saw that the surface of the ground was dry. He waited two more months and at last, the earth was completely dry!

Then God said to Noah, "Come out of the ark. Bring out every kind of living thing that is with you." So Noah, his family, and all the animals finally came out of the ark!

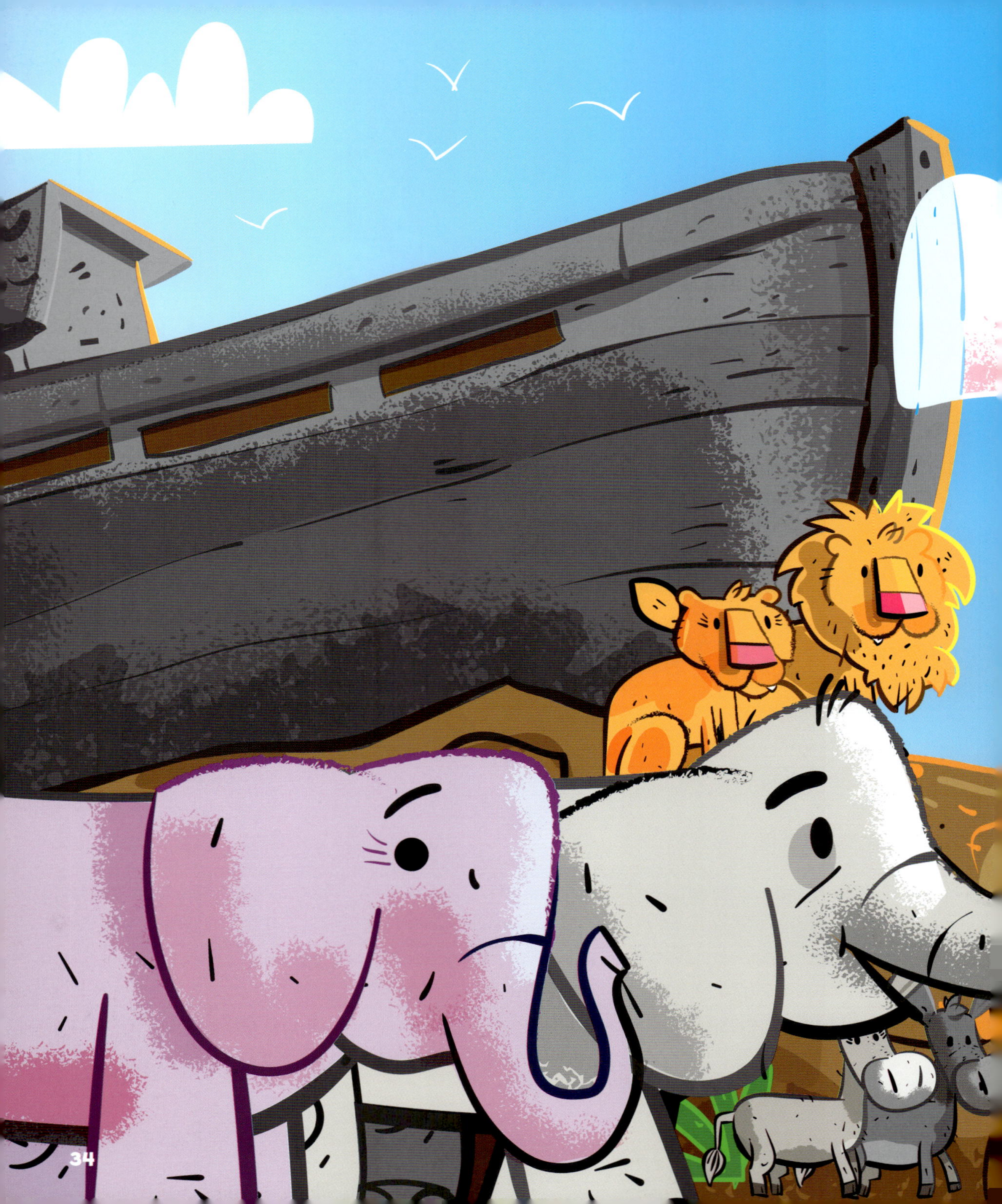

Noah built an altar to honor God and gave an offering to him. God was pleased with Noah's offering. God promised that he would never again send another flood and destroy every living thing on earth. He put a rainbow in the sky as a sign of this promise to Noah, his family, and all life on earth.

God's Promises for Abraham and Sarah

Genesis 13:14-18; 15:1-6; 17:1-22; 18:1-15; 21:1-16

This is Abram, and he was married to Sarai. When they lived in Canaan, God told Abram he would give him all the land he could see and that Abram would have as many children as there are stars in the sky. God said he would bless Abram's family and they would be a blessing to all people.

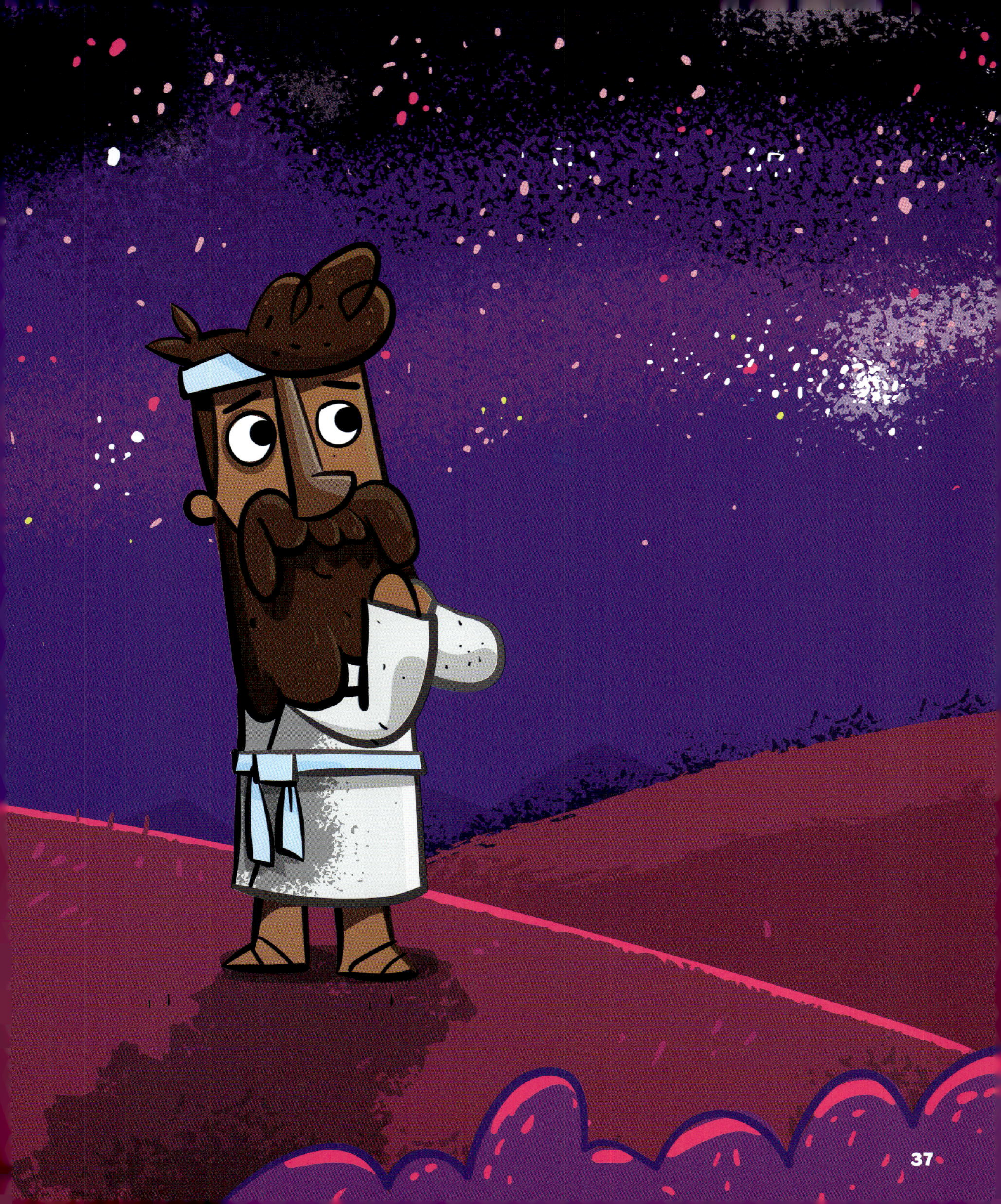

Many years passed. Abram and Sarai were very old and still had no children. God appeared to Abram again and told him his name would now be Abraham, which means "father of many nations." God also changed Sarai's name to Sarah and promised to bless Sarah with a son.

One day Abraham was sitting at the entrance to his tent during the hottest part of the day when the Lord appeared to him. Abraham saw three men standing nearby, and he went to welcome them.

He asked them to stay with him for a while to rest and eat. The men agreed. So Abraham had Sarah and his servant prepare food for the men. When the food was ready, Abraham took the food and served it.

The men asked him, "Where is your wife Sarah?"

Abraham said, "Over there in the tent."

Then one of them said, "I will surely return to you about this time next year, and Sarah your wife will have a son."

Sarah was listening to this from the tent. She laughed to herself because she thought it was funny to think that she and Abraham could have a child in their old age.

Then the Lord said to Abraham, "Why did Sarah laugh? Is anything too hard for me?"

Sarah was afraid. So she lied and said, "I didn't laugh."

But the Lord said, "Yes, you laughed."

A year later, Sarah did have a son. They named him Isaac. God's promises came true for Abraham and Sarah. Abraham became the father of many nations, and from his child came children, and from their children, more children, until Abraham's descendants were truly more than the stars in the sky, just as the Lord had promised.

Jacob and Esau

Genesis 25:19-34; 27-28:5; 29:9-13; 31:2-3; 32-33:11

This is Jacob, who was later called Israel. Jacob was the father of 12 sons. From these 12 sons came the 12 tribes of Israel. Jacob had a twin brother named Esau. Even when Jacob and Esau were in their mother's belly, they fought.

As the boys grew up, Esau liked to be outside and to hunt, while Jacob was quiet and liked to stay home. Esau was their father, Isaac's, favorite because Isaac liked eating what Esau hunted. Jacob was his mother, Rebekah's, favorite.

Esau had a birthright, which meant he would get a special inheritance because he was the firstborn.

One day Jacob was making a stew and Esau came home hungry. Jacob said he would trade Esau some stew for his birthright. Esau was so hungry that he agreed, and Jacob was given Esau's birthright.

Later on, Isaac was getting very old and he wanted to bless his son Esau. Isaac's blessing was very important, and Rebekah wanted Jacob to have the blessing instead of Esau. So, Rebekah told Jacob to pretend to be Esau and go to his father for the blessing. Isaac wasn't able to see anymore, so he believed that Jacob was Esau and blessed him.

Esau came to his father to get his blessing, but Isaac had already given it to Jacob. Esau was angry with Jacob, and he made plans to kill his brother. Rebekah heard of this and had Isaac send Jacob away to live with her family.

For many years, Jacob lived with his uncle and worked in the fields taking care of his flock. He started a family and gained many servants, cattle, donkeys, sheep, and goats. God told Jacob to leave his uncle's land and go back to the land of his father.

So, Jacob took his family and everything he owned and traveled back home. Jacob knew his brother would be there, and he heard that Esau had an army of 400 men with him! Jacob prayed to God and asked God to rescue him from Esau. Then he sent gifts for his brother.

That night Jacob was alone in his camp, for he had sent his family and everything he had ahead of him.

A man came and wrestled with him until dawn. The man saw that he couldn't win. So he struck Jacob's hip and dislocated it. He said, "Let me go." But Jacob said, "I won't let you go unless you bless me."

Then the man gave Jacob a new name. He said, "From now on you will be called Israel, because you have fought with God and men and have won." The man blessed Jacob. Jacob left that place, but he had a limp because of the injury to his hip.

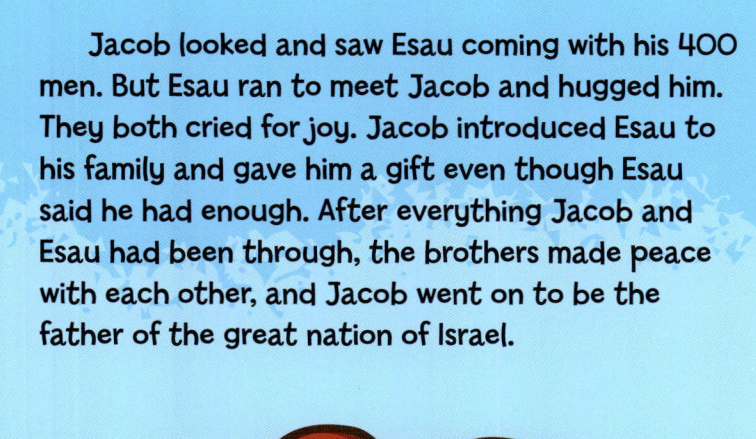

Jacob looked and saw Esau coming with his 400 men. But Esau ran to meet Jacob and hugged him. They both cried for joy. Jacob introduced Esau to his family and gave him a gift even though Esau said he had enough. After everything Jacob and Esau had been through, the brothers made peace with each other, and Jacob went on to be the father of the great nation of Israel.

Joseph's Coat
Genesis 37

This is Joseph. Joseph was the son of Israel, also called Jacob, and Rachel. Israel loved Joseph more than all his other sons. In fact, he made Joseph a coat of many colors to show him how much he loved him. When Joseph's brothers saw this, they hated Joseph.

55

One night Joseph had a dream. Joseph told his brothers, "Listen to the dream I had. We were tying up bundles of grain out in the field. Suddenly my bundle stood up straight. Your bundles gathered around my bundle and bowed down to it." This made his brothers hate Joseph even more, and they said, "Will you really rule over us?"

Then Joseph had another dream, and he told his brothers and his father, "I had another dream. This time the sun and moon and 11 stars were bowing down to me."

This time Israel heard the dream and rebuked Joseph, saying, "Will we really come and bow down to the ground in front of you?" The brothers were jealous of Joseph. Israel, however, decided to think about what Joseph had said.

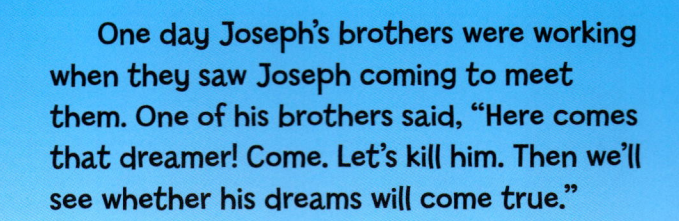

One day Joseph's brothers were working when they saw Joseph coming to meet them. One of his brothers said, "Here comes that dreamer! Come. Let's kill him. Then we'll see whether his dreams will come true."

Joseph's brother Reuben wanted to save Joseph, so he said, "Let us not take his life. Throw him into this empty well here in the desert." So when Joseph came to his brothers, they attacked him. They took the coat their father had given Joseph and threw him into the well.

Then they saw a group of men from Midian coming toward them. Judah thought it would be a good idea to sell Joseph to these men. So the brothers sold Joseph to the traders for 20 shekels.

The brothers then took the coat of many colors back to their father and made him think that Joseph had been killed. Israel wept for his beloved son.

Meanwhile, Joseph was taken as a slave to Egypt to work in the house of a man named Potiphar, one of Pharaoh's officials and the captain of the guard.

Joseph's story was only just beginning.

Joseph Forgives His Brothers
Genesis 39:20-23; 41-45:15; 50:20

Joseph, the son of Israel and Rachel, was hated by his brothers and sold into slavery. Joseph was put in jail even though he had done nothing wrong! But Joseph was good at telling people what their dreams meant. He even told Pharaoh what Pharaoh's dreams meant about the future of Egypt. He predicted that Egypt would have seven years with plenty of food, followed by seven years of famine. Because of this, Pharaoh made Joseph a leader in his kingdom.

Just as Joseph had said, Egypt had seven years with plenty of food. But Joseph knew this time would come to an end, so he made a plan to store extra grain. Then the seven years of famine began. The Egyptians had food to eat because of Joseph's plan. But there wasn't enough food in all the other lands, and many people came to Egypt to buy food.

When Israel heard there was food in Egypt, he sent his sons to buy some. But Israel did not send his youngest son Benjamin with the others. He was afraid he might get hurt.

Egypt

Home

N W E S

When Joseph's brothers came to him, Joseph recognized them but he pretended to be a stranger. Joseph decided to test his brothers. He sent one of them back to get Benjamin.

Then he put his other brothers in prison for three days. On the third day, Joseph let all but one of the brothers take grain back to Canaan with the instruction to bring Benjamin back with them.

The brothers traveled home to their father and stayed there until all the grain was gone. Then they brought Benjamin back with them to Egypt to get more food.

When Joseph saw Benjamin, he was deeply moved at seeing his brother. He released the brother who was still in prison.

Joseph sent the brothers away but told his servant to hide his silver cup in Benjamin's bag. Then Joseph told the servant to go after the brothers and get the cup back. The brothers hadn't traveled far before the servant stopped them and found the cup in Benjamin's bag.

The brothers went back to Joseph and bowed down to him. Joseph's brother, Judah, asked to be punished instead of Benjamin for taking the cup.

Joseph finally told his brothers who he really was. He told them of all that had happened to him in Egypt. For his brothers had intended to harm Joseph, but God intended it all for good. God brought Joseph to Egypt so he could save the lives of many people.

Baby Moses
Exodus 1-2:10

This is Moses. Moses was an Israelite boy born in Egypt at a time when Israelite boys were in great danger.

Pharaoh made the Israelites slaves. He made them work long, hard hours building up Egyptian cities. But even though he tried to stop the Israelites from growing in number and strength, they did. So Pharaoh made a rule that no Israelite boy would be allowed to live.

When Moses was born, his mother saw that he was special, and she hid him for three months. But when she couldn't hide him any longer, she made a basket and put him on the bank of the Nile River among the reeds.

Moses' sister Miriam stayed to watch what would happen to her baby brother.

Soon Pharaoh's daughter came to the edge of the river. When she saw the basket, she sent her servant to get it.

When she saw the baby, she realized he must be an Israelite, and she felt sorry for him.

Then Miriam went to Pharaoh's daughter and asked if she would like her to find an Israelite woman to take care of the baby. Pharaoh's daughter said yes. So Miriam got her mother.

Moses' own mother took care of him until he was old enough to live in Pharaoh's house, where Pharaoh's daughter adopted him as her son. And so Moses, an Israelite boy who wasn't supposed to be alive, became the adopted grandson of Pharaoh.

Moses and the Red Sea
Exodus 2:11-15; 7-14

Moses grew up in the palace of Pharaoh, the very man who made the Israelite people slaves. When Moses grew up, he made a wrong decision and ran away to the land of Midian.

Many years later, God spoke to Moses through a burning bush. God told Moses to go back to Egypt to rescue God's people with the help of his brother Aaron.

Pharaoh's heart was hardened and he did not want to let God's people go, so God showed his power throughout all of Egypt by sending ten plagues. On the night of the last plague, Pharaoh woke up and heard a great cry in Egypt, for there was not an Egyptian house in which someone was not dead.

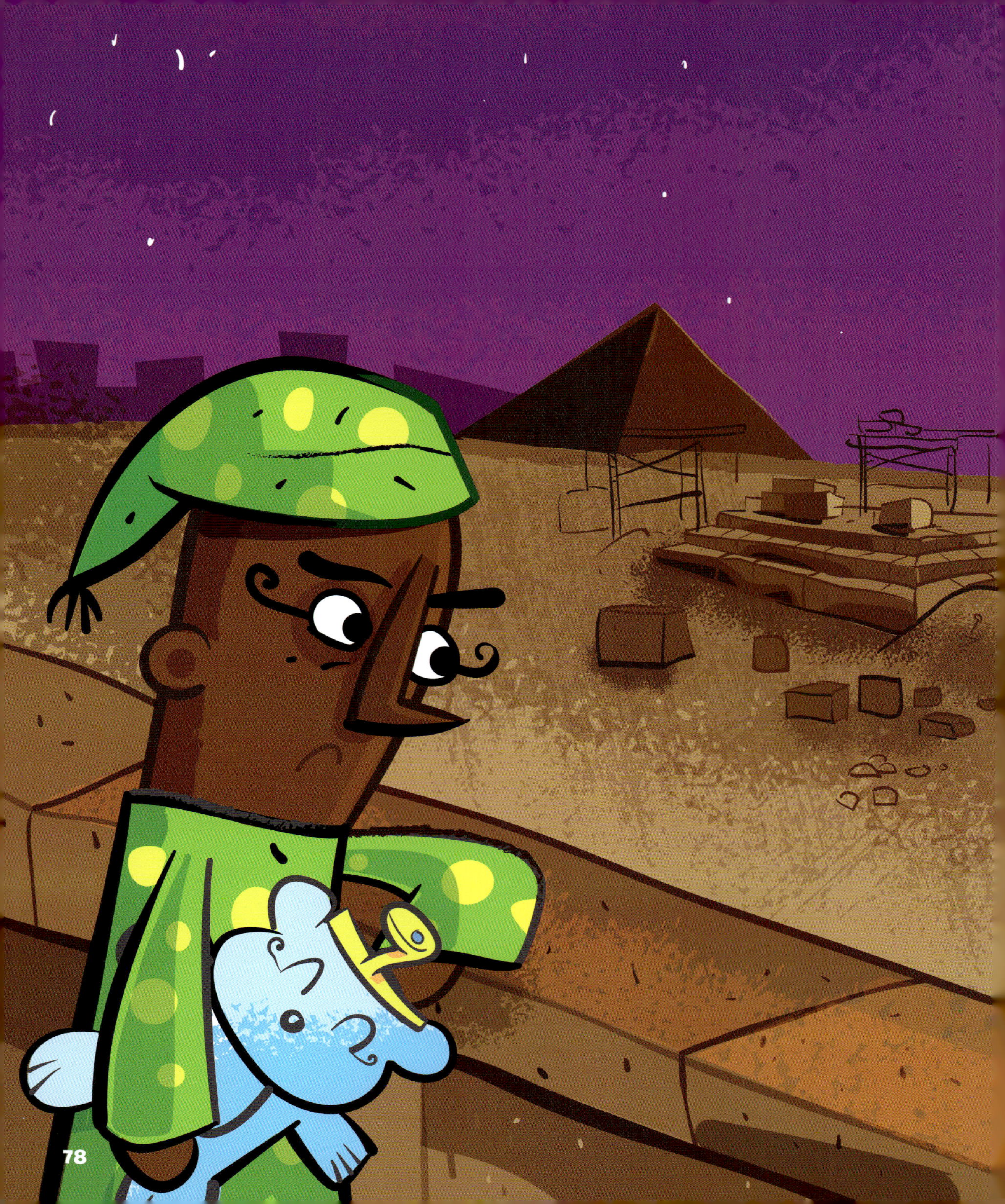

Pharaoh called for Moses and Aaron and told them to leave Egypt with the Israelites. So the Israelites immediately left Egypt and made their way toward the promised land. God led the Israelites as a pillar of fire by night and a cloud by day.

God told Moses to have the people camp along the shore of the Red Sea. He told Moses the Egyptians would come after them, but that God would show his glory and power through this. When word reached Pharaoh that the Israelites had gone, Pharaoh changed his mind and readied his army to take the Israelites back to Egypt.

The Egyptians found the Israelites camped along the shore of the sea. As Pharaoh and his armies came close, the Israelites were terrified! They cried out to God and asked Moses, "What have you done to us by bringing us out of Egypt?"

But Moses told the people, "Don't be afraid. The Lord himself will fight for you. Just be still."

Then God said to Moses, "Tell the people to get moving!" As night came, the pillar of cloud became fire and it went between the Israelites and the Egyptians.

God told Moses to reach out his hand over the Red Sea. Moses did, and God pushed a path through the water with a strong wind. God turned the sea into dry land. The people of Israel went through the sea on dry ground. There was a wall of water on their right side and on their left.

83

The Egyptians chased after the Israelites. When all the Israelites had reached the other side, God said to Moses, "Reach out your hand over the sea." Moses did, and the sea went back to its place. The Egyptians tried to run back, but God swept them into the sea.

That is how God rescued Israel from the Egyptians. That day, the Israelites saw the amazing power of God, and they trusted God and his servant Moses.

The Ten Commandments
Exodus 1:21; Deuteronomy 5

When the Israelites were in the desert, God gave them a special set of rules called the Ten Commandments. The people were afraid to hear from God. So God spoke these commandments to Moses, and Moses told the people.

Then God wrote the commandments on two stone tablets and gave them to Moses. God told Moses that he must teach the people to obey the rules and do all that God had commanded. When the Israelites followed God's commandments, they would show the world they lived differently than all the others and that they were God's chosen people.

1. Do not put any other gods in place of me.
2. Do not worship false gods.
3. Do not misuse the name of God.
4. Remember the sabbath day.
5. Honor your father and mother.

6   Do not murder.

7   Do not commit adultery.

8   Do not steal.

9   Do not tell lies about your neighbor.

10 Do not covet anything your neighbor owns.

Joshua and Caleb

Numbers 12-14:38; Joshua 1:1-10

This is Joshua, and this is Caleb. Joshua and Caleb were two Israelites who followed Moses out of Egypt.

God told Moses to send a leader from each of the 12 tribes of Israel to check out the promised land, which was called the land of Canaan. Joshua and Caleb were among them. Moses told them to go see what the land was like and find out if the people living there were strong or weak.

So the 12 men went and checked out the land. While they were there, they found a single cluster of grapes that took two men to carry!

After 40 days, they returned to Moses and showed them the fruit they found. They said it was a land with plenty of milk and honey, and that it was a good land. But they also said the people living there were powerful and that their cities were strong. They even saw giants there!

Caleb said, "We should go up and take the land. We can certainly do it." But the other men who had gone to Canaan spread a bad report throughout the Israelite camp that scared the Israelites.

They told Moses and Aaron they wished they had died in Egypt or in the wilderness. They asked for a new leader who would take them back to Egypt. But Joshua and Caleb told the people, "If the Lord is pleased with us, he'll lead us into that land. He'll give it to us. But don't refuse to obey him. And don't be afraid of the people of the land. The Lord is with us. So nothing can save them."

But the Israelites talked about hurting Joshua and Caleb.

Then God appeared and spoke to Moses. He was angry at the Israelites and said, "Will they never believe me, even after all the miraculous signs I have done among them?" God said he would make a new nation from Moses and that the Israelites would be no more, but Moses asked God to forgive his people. God said he would, but the Israelites would wander in the wilderness for 40 more years, and none of the older people would enter the promised land except for Joshua and Caleb.

The people did wander for 40 years. Moses died, and Joshua became the new leader of the Israelites. The time came for Joshua to lead the Israelites into the promised land that Joshua and Caleb had scouted many years before.

The Israelites Cross the Jordan
Joshua 3-4

This is Joshua. Joshua was the leader of the Israelites who led God's people into the promised land.

Joshua readied God's people to cross the Jordan River, which was the only thing between the Israelites and the land that God had promised them.

They camped beside the river for three days waiting, just as the Lord had commanded them. At this time of year, the Jordan River was overflowing with so much water that it was impossible to cross on foot.

God told Joshua to have the priests carry the ark of the covenant to the river and stand in the river.

As soon as the priests did this, the water of the Jordan stopped flowing, and the priests stood with the ark of the covenant on dry ground as the Israelites crossed to the other side.

God told Joshua to send 12 men from the 12 tribes of Israel to take 12 stones from the place that the priests were standing.

When all this had been finished as God commanded, Joshua called the priests from the Jordan. As the priests' feet left the Jordan River, the water came back into place just as it had been.

They brought the stones to their camp and set them as a memorial so future generations might remember the story of how God brought his people through the Jordan River on dry ground.

The Walls of Jericho
Joshua 2; 5:13-6:27

God told Joshua it was time to take the promised land. So Joshua sent spies into the city of Jericho. While those spies were in Jericho, they were protected by a woman named Rahab. The spies promised to save Rahab and her family when they took the land. And Rahab hung a scarlet cord from her window to remind them of their promise.

Now the Israelites had crossed the Jordan and were camped near Jericho. The commander of the Lord's army appeared to Joshua to deliver God's message. The Lord said that he wanted Joshua to take the city of Jericho, but that Joshua needed to follow his instructions exactly.

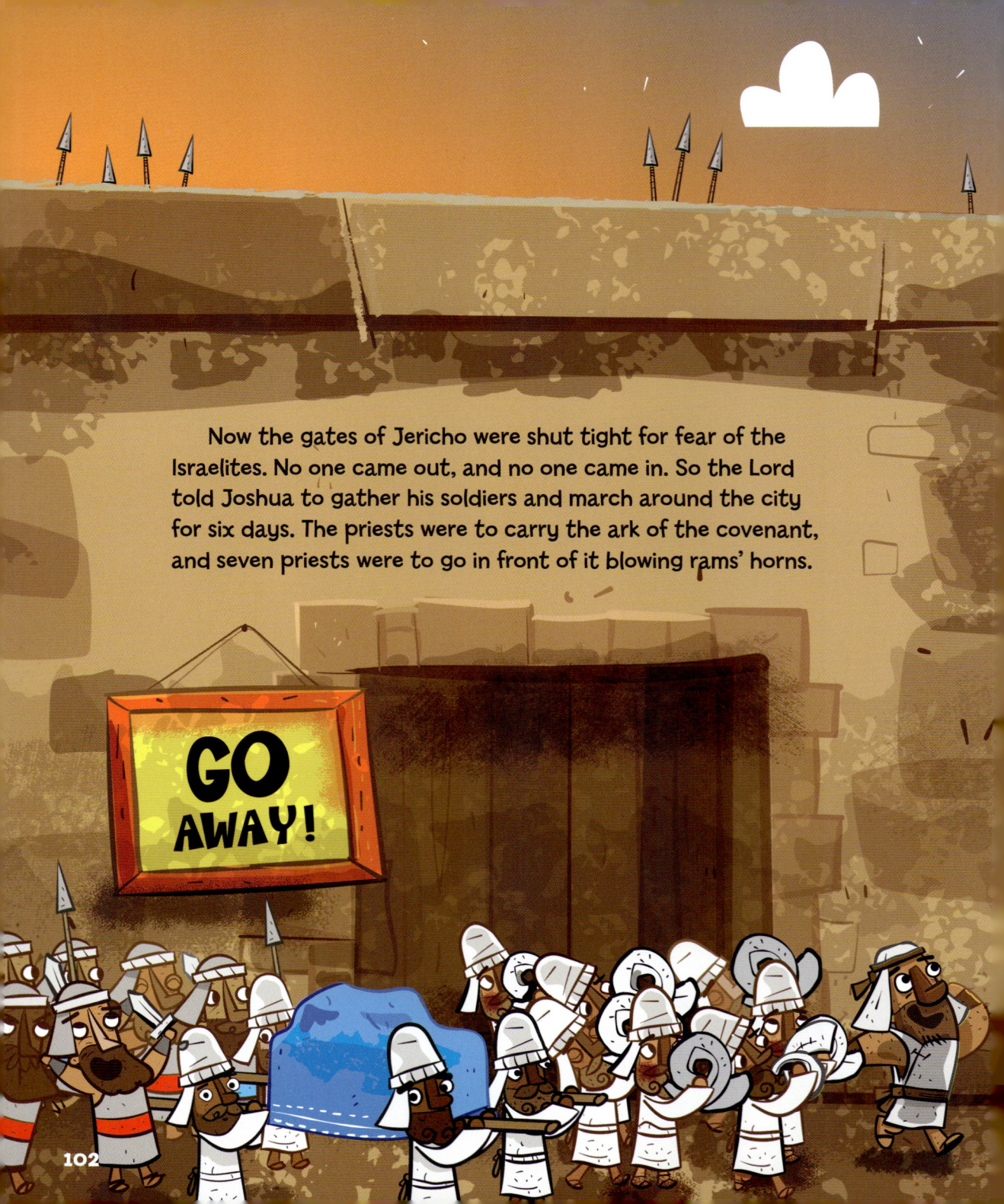

Now the gates of Jericho were shut tight for fear of the Israelites. No one came out, and no one came in. So the Lord told Joshua to gather his soldiers and march around the city for six days. The priests were to carry the ark of the covenant, and seven priests were to go in front of it blowing rams' horns.

GO AWAY!

On the seventh day they were to march around the city seven times and blow the horn.

Joshua and the Israelites did all this, and then Joshua said, "Shout! The Lord has given you the city!"

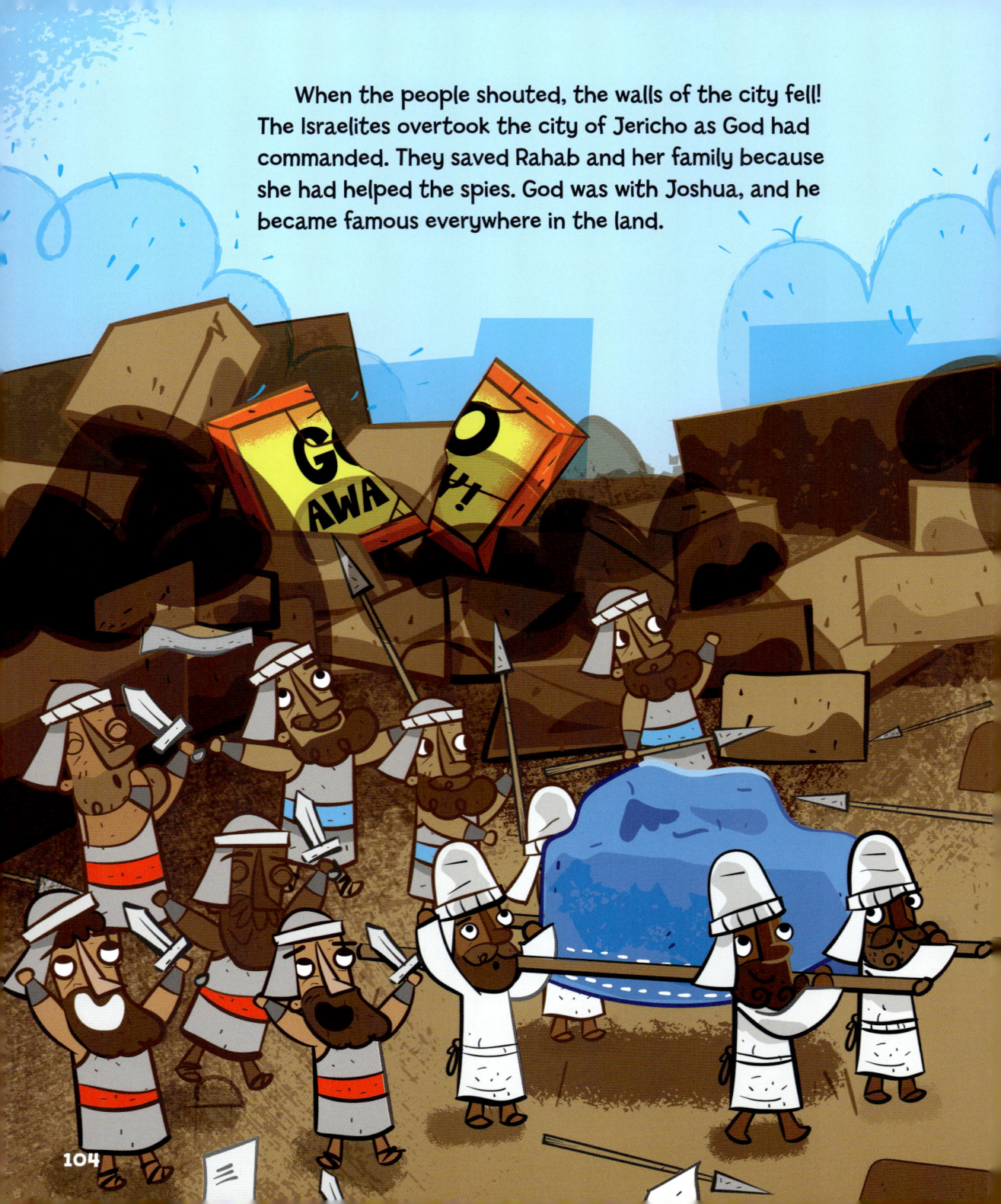

When the people shouted, the walls of the city fell! The Israelites overtook the city of Jericho as God had commanded. They saved Rahab and her family because she had helped the spies. God was with Joshua, and he became famous everywhere in the land.

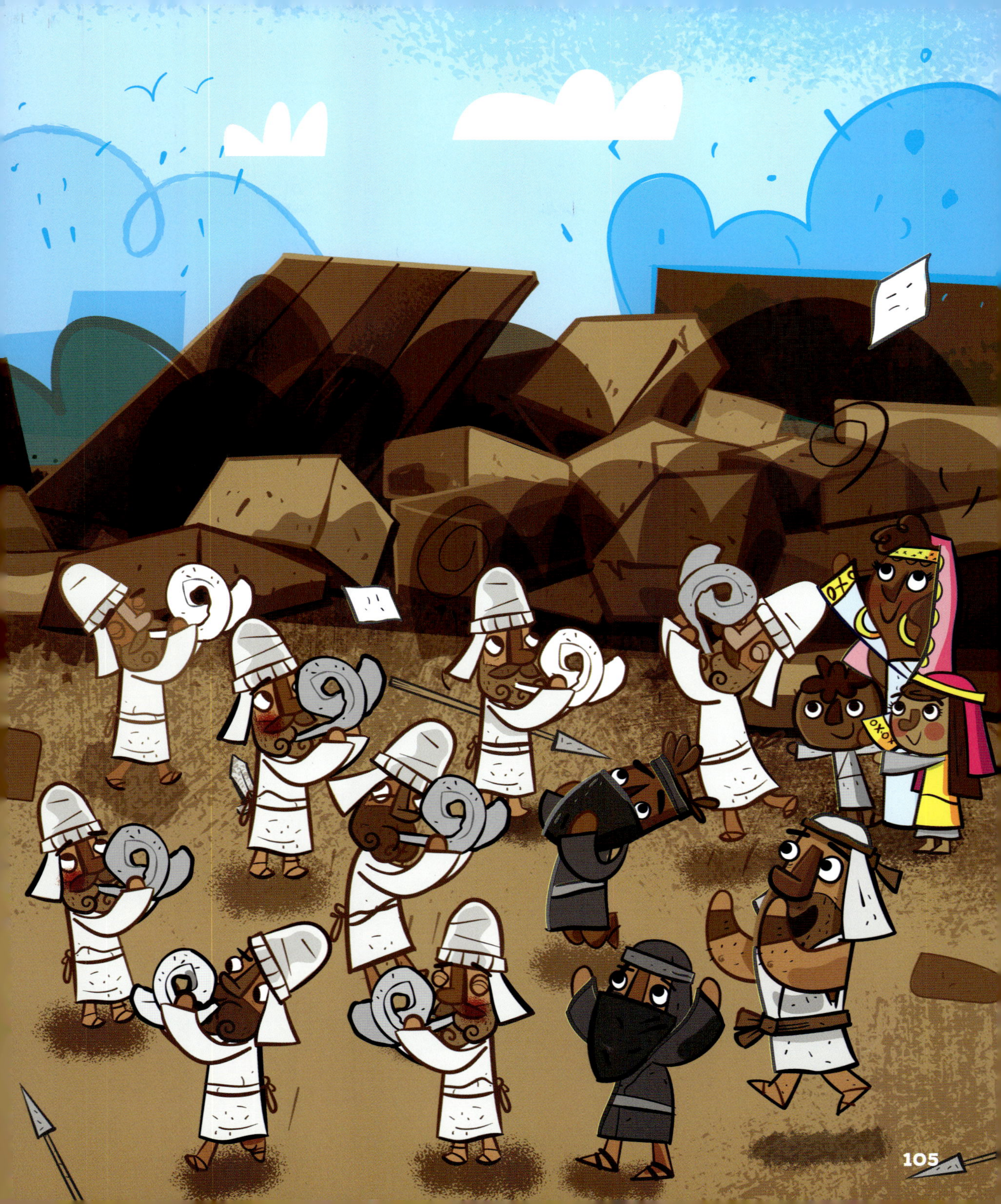

Gideon's 300 Men
Judges 7

This is Gideon, who was a judge of Israel. Judges were men and women God chose to lead his people from the time of Joshua until they asked for a king. In the time when Gideon lived, the Israelites were being treated badly by a group called the Midianites. The Midianites took all their food and ruined the land. The Israelites cried out to God and asked him to help. God chose Gideon to rescue the Israelites.

Early one morning, Gideon and his army came close to the Midianite camp. God said to Gideon, "I want to hand Midian over to you. But you have too many men for me to do that. Then Israel might brag, 'My own strength has saved me.'" So God told Gideon to let all the men go except for 300.

Now the Midianite camp was in the valley just below where Gideon and his 300 men were. That night God told Gideon to go down to the camp and listen to what the Midianites were saying. God told Gideon that if he was afraid he could take his servant Purah with him. So Gideon and Purah went to the edge of the enemy camp.

The enemy army was huge! There were too many men and camels for Gideon to even count! Gideon crept up close to the camp and heard a man telling his friend about his dream. The man said that in his dream a loaf of bread came tumbling down to the camp and knocked a tent down flat. His friend said the dream could only mean one thing—that God had handed the Midianites over to Gideon. When Gideon heard this, he worshiped God.

Then he went back to the Israelite camp and shouted, "Get up! The Lord has handed the Midianites over to you." He separated the 300 men into three groups and gave them each a trumpet and a clay jar with a torch in it.

Then he said, "Watch me. Do what I do." So the Israelite army went down to the enemy camp.

It was nighttime, after the guard had been changed. Suddenly, the Israelites blew their trumpets and broke their jars. They held their torches in one hand and trumpets in the other and shouted, "A sword for the Lord and for Gideon!"

Gideon and his 300 men stayed in position around the camp and watched as all the Midianites ran around in fear! Then they blew their trumpets, and God caused the men in the enemy camp to fight against each other. Some of them ran away, but Gideon called for the warriors of the other tribes in Israel to catch them. And so God used Gideon and his army of 300 men to defeat the Midianite army, just as he said he would.

Ruth
Ruth 1-4

This is Naomi, a Jewish woman from Bethlehem in Judah. Naomi's husband took her and their two sons to live in a country called Moab because there wasn't enough food in Judah.

While they were in Moab, Naomi's husband died, and her sons married two Moabite women named Orpah and Ruth. Then Naomi's sons died, leaving Naomi, Orpah, and Ruth alone. Naomi heard that God had helped his people in Judah by giving them good crops for food again. So Naomi left to go back to Judah, and Orpah and Ruth went with her.

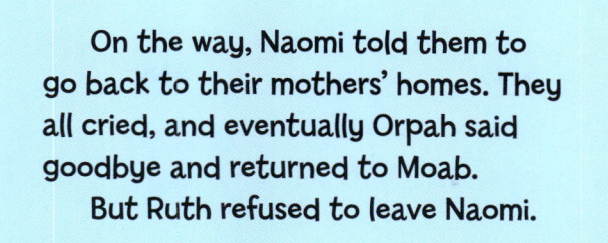

On the way, Naomi told them to go back to their mothers' homes. They all cried, and eventually Orpah said goodbye and returned to Moab.
But Ruth refused to leave Naomi.

She said, "Don't try to make me leave you and go back. Where you go I'll go. Where you stay I'll stay. Your people will be my people. Your God will be my God." Naomi realized that Ruth had made up her mind to go with her, so they traveled to Judah together.

When Ruth and Naomi arrived, it was harvest time in Bethlehem. Ruth went to gather grain in the field of a man named Boaz. Boaz heard of all that Ruth had done for Naomi. He treated Ruth with kindness and made sure that she and Naomi had food from the fields.

Boaz was a close relative of Naomi's husband, so Ruth went to Boaz and asked him to protect her and Naomi by making Ruth his wife. Boaz agreed! Ruth and Boaz got married and had a son named Obed.

Naomi cared for Obed as if he were her own. Obed went on to have a son of his own named Jesse, and Jesse had a son named David. David would be the great king of Israel who defeated a giant named Goliath. And many, many years later Ruth and Boaz's descendants would include Jesus, the Savior of the world!

119

Hannah
1 Samuel 1

This is Hannah. Hannah was married to a man named Elkanah. They were not able to have any children, and this made Hannah very sad.

Every year, Hannah and Elkanah would go to the House of the Lord at Shiloh to worship God and make sacrifices. Hannah told God that if he gave her a son, she would give the child back to him and that her son would serve God all the days of his life.

Hannah was deeply upset and cried as she prayed. Eli, one of the priests, thought the way she was praying was very strange, so he went over to Hannah to stop her. But Hannah explained that she had been praying this way because she was very sad and she was telling God all of her troubles.

Eli said, "May the God of Israel give you what you have asked him for." Hannah wasn't sad anymore.

After some time, Hannah became pregnant and had a baby boy. She named him Samuel for she said, "I asked the Lord for him."

Hannah did as she promised God she would, and once Samuel was a little older, she took him to the House of God. Hannah prayed and gave thanks to God. And Samuel grew up in the House of God, serving the Lord.

God Speaks to Samuel

1 Samuel 3

This is Samuel. Samuel was the son of Hannah. Hannah prayed for God to give her a son, and he did! So Hannah gave Samuel back to God, and Samuel grew up in the House of God. As Samuel grew up, he learned how to serve God from Eli the priest.

Even though Samuel lived in the House of God, he did not know what God's voice sounded like. In those days, God didn't give many messages to his people. Then one night after Eli and Samuel had gone to bed, God suddenly called out to Samuel.

Samuel got up and ran to Eli and said, "Here I am. You called out to me."

Eli said, "I didn't call you. Go back and lie down." So Samuel did.

Then God called out again, "Samuel!" And again Samuel got up and ran to Eli saying, "Here I am. You called out to me."

Eli said, "I didn't call you. Go back and lie down." So Samuel did.

125

God called Samuel for a third time, and Samuel went to Eli yet again.

This time, Eli realized that God was trying to speak to Samuel. So Eli told Samuel to say, "Speak, Lord. I'm listening."

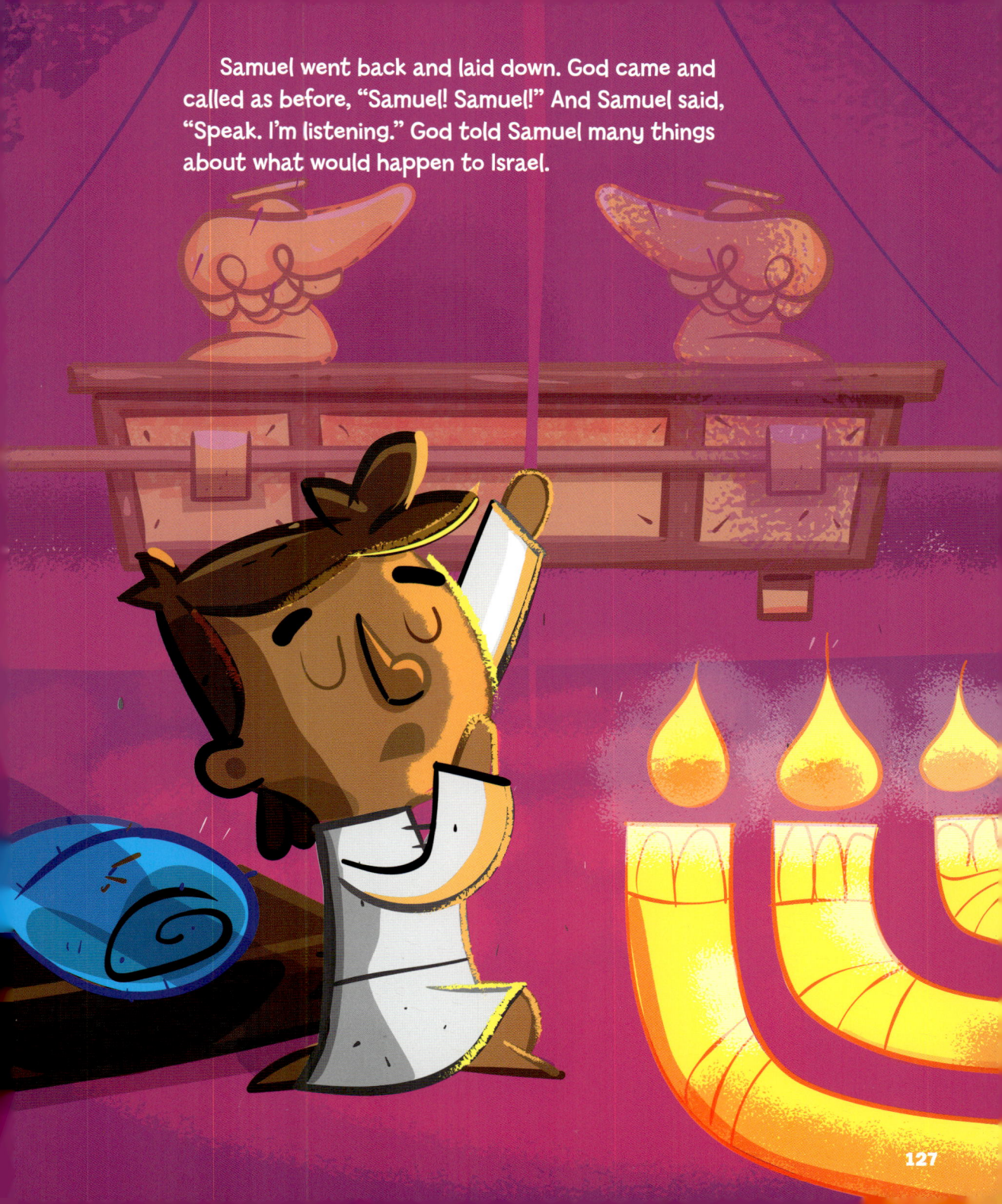

Samuel went back and laid down. God came and called as before, "Samuel! Samuel!" And Samuel said, "Speak. I'm listening." God told Samuel many things about what would happen to Israel.

As Samuel grew up, God was with him and everything God spoke through Samuel came true. Samuel was seen as a great prophet of God because he listened when God spoke to him and told the people what God wanted them to hear.

David Chosen to Be King

1 Samuel 8; 10:1; 15:35; 16:1-13

Israel became a great nation that was ruled by judges, men and women who helped the people follow God. But the people asked for a king so they could be like the other nations. God warned them through the prophet Samuel that a king would not be the best choice for them, but the people wanted a king anyway.

So God chose a man named Saul and had Samuel anoint him. Saul became the king of Israel.

Saul started out as a good king, but he started making wrong choices and did not follow God as he should. God was sad that he made Saul king.

So God sent Samuel to a man named Jesse in Bethlehem because God had chosen one of Jesse's sons to be the new king of Israel.

Jesse's oldest son was strong and handsome. Samuel thought that surely God would choose this son to be king. But God said, "The Lord does not look at the things people look at. People look at the outside of a person. But the Lord looks at what is in the heart."

One by one, Jesse had seven more of his sons walk in front of Samuel. But Samuel said, "The Lord hasn't chosen any of them." Samuel asked if Jesse had any other sons, and Jesse said, "My youngest son is taking care of the sheep."

Samuel asked Jesse to bring the son to him, and Jesse had David brought in from the fields. God said to Samuel, "This is the one."

So Samuel anointed David by pouring oil on his head to show that God had chosen David to be the next king of Israel. From that day on, the Spirit of the Lord came powerfully on David.

David and Goliath
1 Samuel 17:1-50

This is David. David was a shepherd who lived in Israel.

At this time, the Philistines, who were enemies of Israel, were gathering an army to fight King Saul and the Israelite army.

The Philistines had a giant warrior named Goliath. He taunted God's people and said, "Choose one of your men. Have him come down and face me." The Israelites and King Saul were very afraid.

Meanwhile, David's father sent David to bring food to his brothers and their captain. Goliath came out from the Philistine camp, and David heard his taunts.

David said, "He dares the armies of the living God to fight him. Who does he think he is?"

Someone heard what David said and reported it to Saul, who sent for him. David said, "Don't let anyone lose hope because of that Philistine. I'll go out and fight him."

Saul said, "You aren't able to go out there and fight that Philistine. You are too young."

But David told Saul that he had taken care of his father's sheep and saved them from lions and bears. Then David said, "The Lord saved me from the paw of the lion. He saved me from the paw of the bear. And he'll save me from the powerful hand of this Philistine too!"

So Saul said, "Go. And may the Lord be with you."

David picked up five smooth stones from a stream. Then with his sling in hand, he went to face Goliath.

When Goliath saw David coming, he yelled mean things at David. But David said, "You are coming to fight against me with a sword, a spear, and a javelin. But I'm coming against you in the name of the Lord who rules over all."

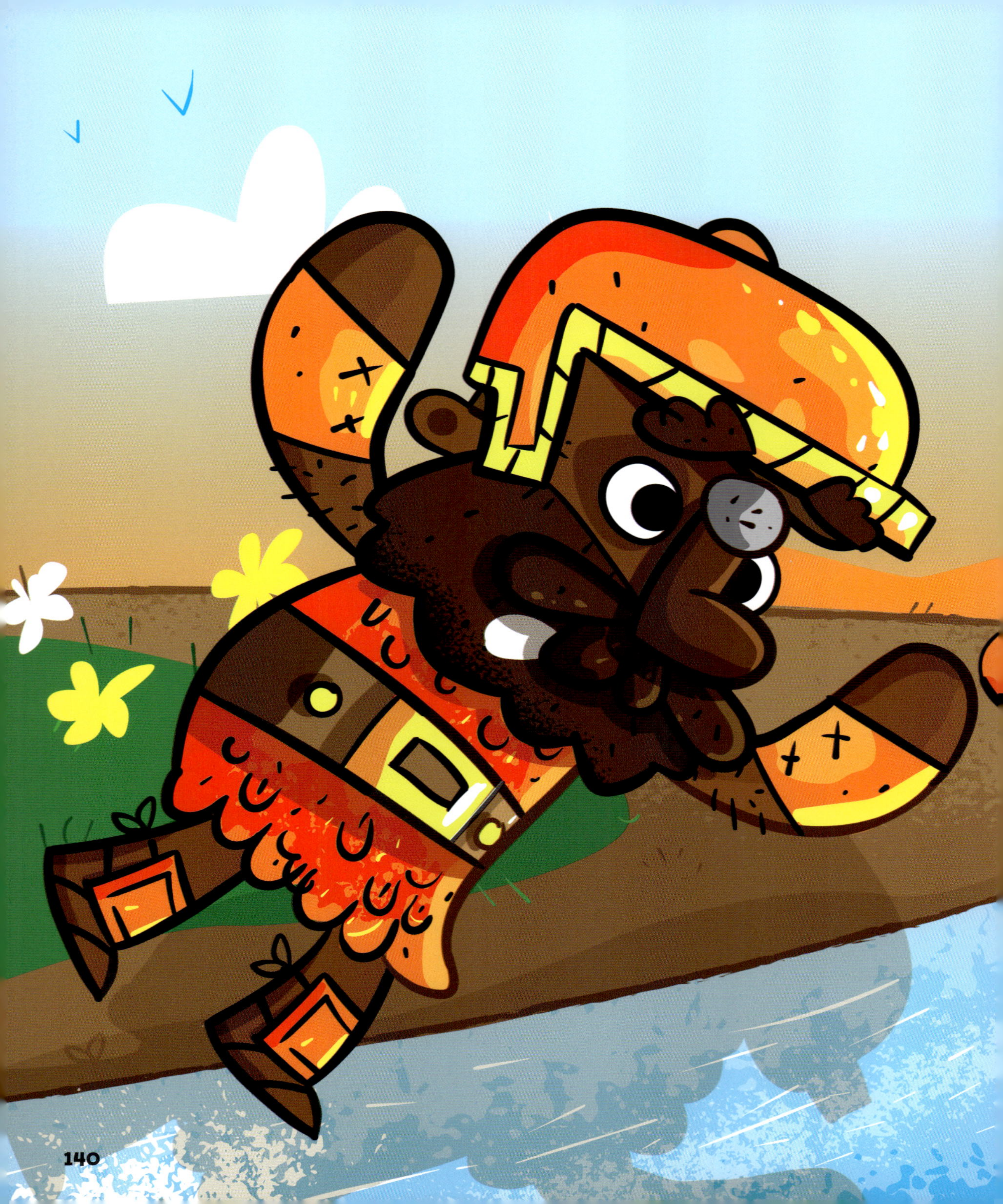

Goliath moved closer to attack, and David ran to meet him. He took out a stone and put it in his sling. He slung it at Goliath, and the stone hit him in the forehead. Goliath fell to the ground.

So David triumphed over the Philistine because he knew the power of God and trusted God to win the battle against the giant.

Solomon Asks for Wisdom

1 Kings 3:3-15; 2 Chronicles 1:7-13

This is Solomon. Solomon became king of Israel after his father David. Solomon loved God, and God made him very powerful.

One night, God appeared to Solomon in a dream. God said, "Ask for anything you want me to give you."

Solomon said, "You were very kind to my father David. Now you have made me king in his place." But Solomon didn't know how to do his job when there were so many people in Israel to lead. So Solomon asked God for wisdom so that he could rule God's people well and know the difference between right and wrong.

God was pleased that Solomon asked for wisdom. It showed that his greatest desire was to do what was right and fair for God's people. God said, "Wisdom and knowledge will be given to you. I will also give you wealth, possessions, and honor. You will have more than any king before you ever had. And no king after you will have as much."

Then Solomon woke up, went back to Jerusalem, and made sacrifices to God. God gave all he said he would to Solomon. Solomon was known as a wise king and ruled God's people with wisdom for many years.

Jehoshaphat
2 Chronicles 20:1-34

This is Jehoshaphat, one of the kings of Judah. He was a good king who made Judah stronger and did what God said was right. He obeyed God's commandments, and God was with him.

There were other countries around Judah who wanted to start a war with Judah. One day messengers came to Jehoshaphat and said that the armies of three kingdoms were marching toward Judah.

Jehoshaphat was terrified by this news and asked God for advice. He told everyone in Judah to start fasting. People from all the towns of Judah came to Jerusalem to ask God for help.

Jehoshaphat stood among the people and prayed to God. He asked for God's help, saying, "Lord, you are the God of our people. You are strong and powerful. No one can fight against you and win. We don't know what to do. But we're looking to you to help us."

All the men of Judah stood before God with their wives and children. The spirit of God came upon one of the men, and he said, "Listen! The Lord says to you, 'Do not be afraid. Do not lose hope because of this huge army. The battle is not yours. It is God's.'" He told them they would march out against the armies, but they would not need to fight, for God would be with them! Then King Jehoshaphat and all the people of Israel worshiped God.

The next morning the army of Judah went out to battle. Jehoshaphat said to them, "Have faith in the Lord your God. He'll take good care of you." Jehoshaphat sent the singers to walk ahead of the army, and they praised God as they led the army.

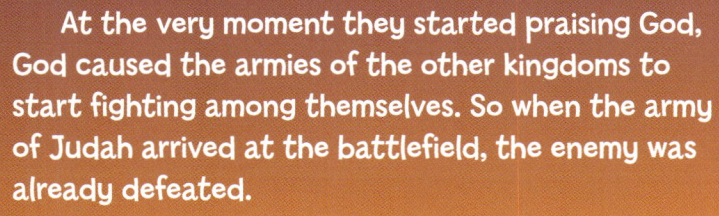

At the very moment they started praising God, God caused the armies of the other kingdoms to start fighting among themselves. So when the army of Judah arrived at the battlefield, the enemy was already defeated.

Jehoshaphat and his men thanked God who had given them victory!

Then they marched into Jerusalem praising God who had defeated their enemies. The kingdom of Judah was at peace.

Josiah
2 Kings 22–23:25

This is Josiah. Josiah became king of Israel when he was only eight years old! Many of the kings before Josiah had made wrong choices, including Josiah's father and grandfather. These kings did not follow God, and they ignored his commandments and his law. But when Josiah became king, he did what God wanted and lived the way King David had lived.

Eighteen years after Josiah became king, he sent his court secretary, Shaphan, to God's temple. Many of the kings before Josiah had not taken good care of God's house, so it needed to be repaired. While they were in the temple, the high priest said to Shaphan, "I've found the Book of the Law in the Lord's temple."

So Shaphan took the Book of the Law back to King Josiah and read it to him. When Josiah heard what was in the book, he was very upset because the people of Israel were not doing the things God asked them to do. Josiah knew that God must be angry with Israel for not obeying God's commandments.

Josiah gathered all the people of Israel at the temple and read the entire Book of the Law to them. That very day Josiah and all the people promised they would obey all of what God commanded with all their hearts and souls.

Josiah helped Israel become fully committed to God. He tore down all of the other temples and the idols they had set up. He got rid of all the people who were doing wrong things throughout Israel. And he did all that was commanded in the Book of the Law.

Never before had there been a king like Josiah, who turned to God with all his heart and soul and strength, obeying all the laws.

Jonah and the Fish

Jonah 1-3

This is Jonah. Jonah was a prophet, so it was his job to tell people what God told him. One day, God told Jonah to go to Nineveh because the people there were doing wrong things.

But instead, Jonah boarded a ship going in the other direction. He was running away from God.

While he was at sea, God sent a strong and powerful wind that caused a storm so big it seemed like it would break the ship apart. All the sailors were afraid. They tried everything they could think of to save the ship.

Meanwhile, Jonah was sound asleep. So the captain went down and said, "How can you sleep? Get up and call out to your god for help! Maybe he'll pay attention to what's happening to us."

Then the sailors figured out that Jonah was the reason for the storm. They asked him, "Who are you? What terrible thing have you done to bring all this trouble on us?"

Jonah told them who he was and that he worshiped the one true God who made the sea. Then he told the sailors to throw him into the sea so the storm would stop.

The sailors still tried to escape the storm, but it was no use.

So they asked God for forgiveness and threw Jonah into the sea. The stormy sea became calm. The sailors were amazed at God's power, and they promised to serve God.

God sent a huge fish to swallow Jonah. Jonah was in the belly of the fish for three days. Jonah prayed to God from inside the fish, and God commanded the fish to spit Jonah out.

God told Jonah again, "Go to the great city of Nineveh."

162

This time Jonah obeyed God and went to Nineveh to deliver God's message. The people of Nineveh stopped doing wrong things and called out to God. They were saved because they listened to the message that God had given Jonah.

Elijah on Mount Carmel

1 Kings 18:1-2, 15-39

This is Elijah. Elijah was a prophet of God in Israel during the reign of King Ahab. Ahab was a terrible king. He led the Israelites to do evil things. They stopped following God and started worshiping a fake god called Baal.

God told Elijah to go speak with Ahab. Elijah told Ahab to bring all of Israel and the prophets of Baal to join him on Mount Carmel. Ahab did as Elijah asked.

Then Elijah asked for two bulls and told the prophets of Baal to choose one to sacrifice to Baal. He told them to put it on the altar but not light it on fire. Elijah then prepared the other bull, but he didn't light his altar on fire either. Then Elijah said, "Pray to your god. And I'll pray to the Lord. The god who answers by sending fire down is the one and only God." And all the people agreed to the test.

Elijah let the prophets of Baal go first. They called on the name of Baal from morning until noon, shouting, "Baal! Answer us!" But no one answered.

Elijah began to tease them. "Shout louder! Perhaps he's away on a trip. Maybe he's sleeping. You might have to wake him up." So they shouted louder and tried with all their might until the evening. But no one answered.

Then Elijah said to all the people, "Come here to me." They went to him as he dug a ditch around the altar. Then he had some men pour water on the altar three times.

Elijah walked up to the altar and prayed to God. "Today let everyone know that you are God in Israel. Let them know I'm your servant. Answer me, Lord. Then these people will know that you are the one and only God."

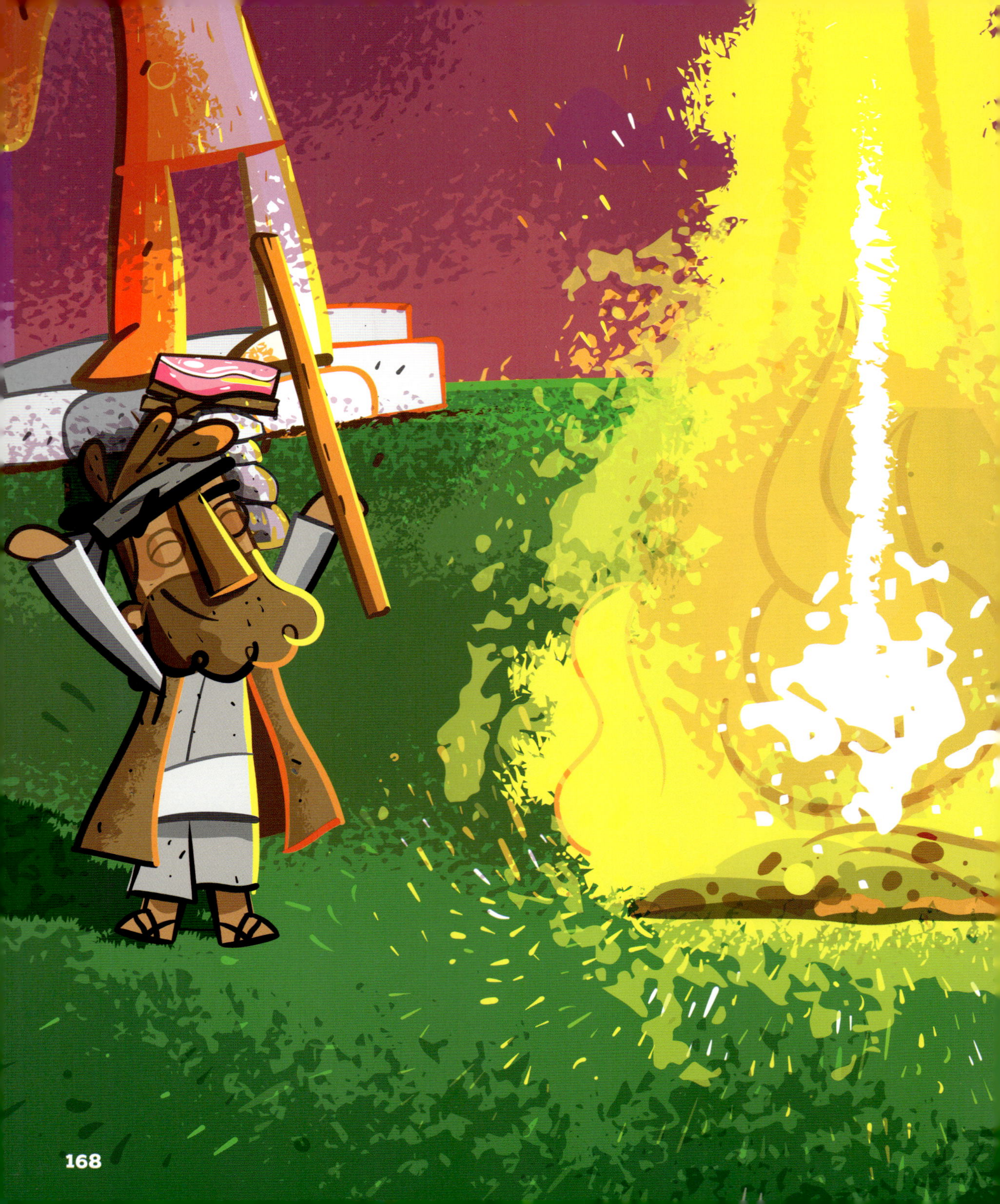

The fire of God came down and burned up the sacrifice, the wood, the stones, the soil, and all the water in the ditch! And when all the people saw it, they fell to the ground and cried out, "The Lord is the one and only God!"

Naaman is Healed
2 Kings 5:1-19

This is Naaman, who was a great leader in Aram's army. Naaman was a brave warrior, but he had leprosy, which gave him sores all over his skin. One of Naaman's servants was a young girl taken from Israel. One day, the girl told Naaman's wife, "I wish my master would go and see the prophet who is in Samaria. He would heal my master of leprosy."

So Naaman went to the king of Aram and told him what the young girl had said. The king told him to go see the prophet and gave him a letter to give the king of Israel. Naaman went to Israel and brought the letter, along with many gifts.

When the king of Israel read the letter, he became very upset because he knew he couldn't heal Naaman. He thought the king of Aram was trying to pick a fight with him. But there was a prophet in Israel named Elisha, who had done many miracles through God's power. When Elisha heard that the king of Israel was upset, he sent him a message that said, "Tell the man to come to me. Then he will know there is a prophet in Israel."

So Naaman went to Elisha's house. But Elisha sent a messenger out to him with this message: "Go! Wash yourself in the Jordan River seven times. Then your skin will be healed."

Naaman was angry that Elisha wouldn't come to meet him. He wanted Elisha to wave his hand over him and ask God to heal him. He didn't understand why he needed to wash in a river in Israel.

But his servants encouraged Naaman to do what Elisha said.

So Naaman went down to the Jordan River and dipped himself seven times, as Elisha had told him to do. His skin became as healthy as a child's, and he was healed!

Naaman went back to find Elisha. Naaman said to Elisha, "Now I know that there is no God anywhere in the whole world except in Israel."

Naaman promised he would only offer sacrifices to the one true God from then on.

Elisha said, "Go in peace." Naaman went home, healed from his leprosy by the power of God.

The Fiery Furnace
Daniel 3

There once were three Jewish men named Shadrach, Meshach, and Abednego. When they were very young, they were taken from Israel to live in a place called Babylon. Babylon's king, Nebuchadnezzar, made a gold statue and declared that everyone would bow down and worship the statue when they heard the sound of musical instruments. Anyone who refused would be thrown into a fiery furnace.

The instruments sounded, and all the people bowed down and worshiped the statue. But Shadrach, Meshach, and Abednego did not. They would only bow to the one, true God. When the king heard that Shadrach, Meshach, and Abednego refused to bow to the statue, he became very angry. He gave the men one more chance to bow down so they wouldn't be thrown into the fire.

But Shadrach, Meshach, and Abednego refused. They said, "We might be thrown into the blazing furnace. But the God we serve is able to bring us out of it alive. He will save us from your power. But we want you to know this, Your Majesty. Even if we knew that our God wouldn't save us, we still wouldn't serve your gods. We wouldn't worship the gold statue you set up."

The king was so angry with Shadrach, Meshach, and Abednego that he ordered the furnace to be heated seven times hotter than usual. Then he ordered Shadrach, Meshach, and Abednego to be tied up and thrown in the fire. The fire was so hot that it killed the soldiers who threw them in.

Suddenly, the king jumped up and said, "Didn't we throw three men into the fire? Look! I see four men walking around in the fire! They aren't tied up. And the fourth man looks like a son of the gods!" Then the king shouted to Shadrach, Meshach, and Abednego, "Come out!"

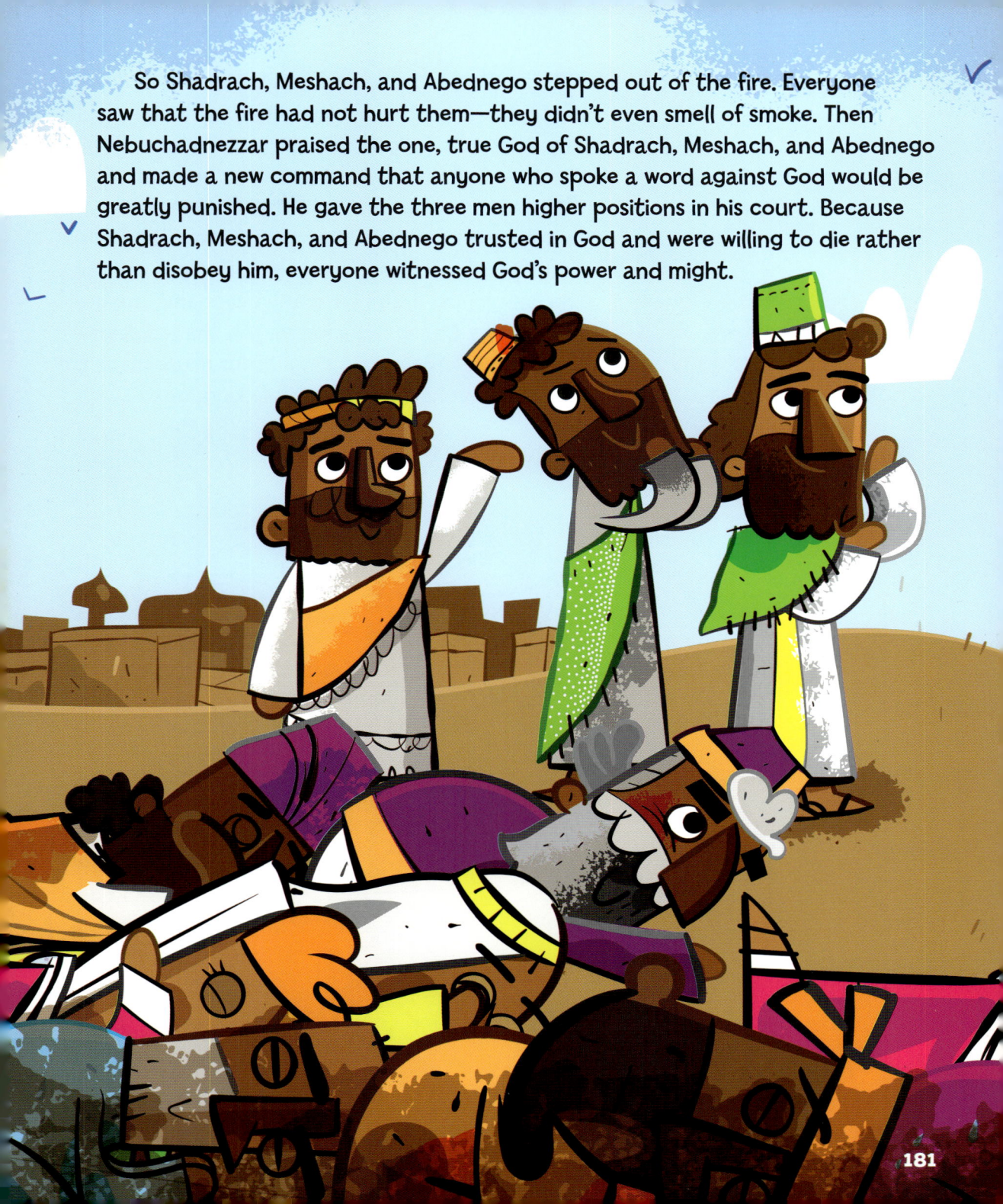

So Shadrach, Meshach, and Abednego stepped out of the fire. Everyone saw that the fire had not hurt them—they didn't even smell of smoke. Then Nebuchadnezzar praised the one, true God of Shadrach, Meshach, and Abednego and made a new command that anyone who spoke a word against God would be greatly punished. He gave the three men higher positions in his court. Because Shadrach, Meshach, and Abednego trusted in God and were willing to die rather than disobey him, everyone witnessed God's power and might.

Daniel in the Lions' Den
Daniel 1; 2:1, 25-30, 46-49; 6

This is Daniel. He was a Jewish man who was taken to Babylon when he was very young. Daniel loved God and followed God's rules. He once showed the power of God's rules by eating the foods God said to, and he gained favor with the king by helping the king understand his dreams. Daniel prayed to God three times a day. Daniel served in the Babylonian court for many years and under many kings. Daniel did a better job than all the other court officials. So King Darius made plans to place him in charge of the whole kingdom.

The other court officials tried to find something wrong with Daniel, but they couldn't. He always followed God and did what he was supposed to. So they went to King Darius and convinced him to make a new law that people could only pray to King Darius. Anyone caught praying to God would be thrown into the lions' den.

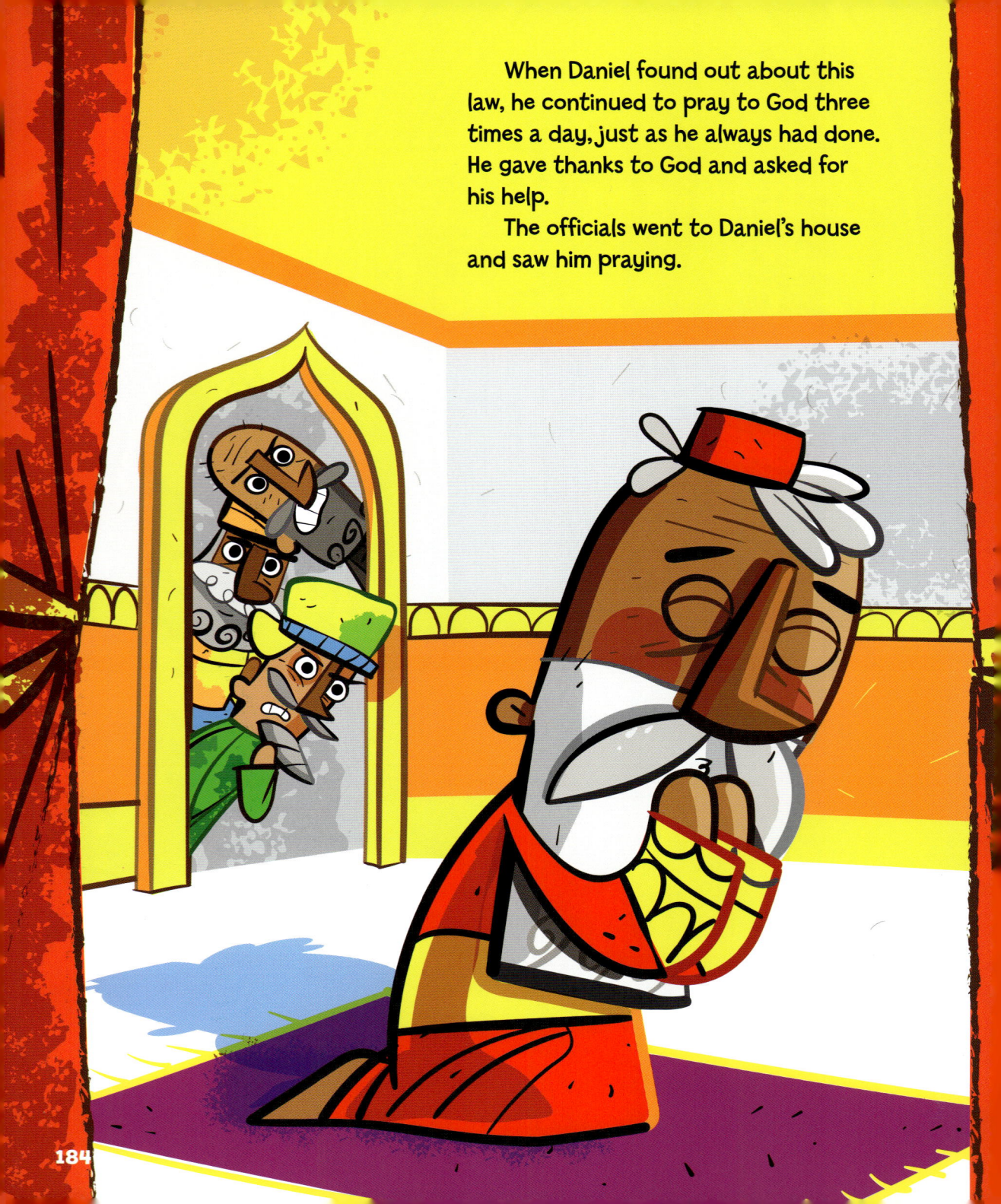

When Daniel found out about this law, he continued to pray to God three times a day, just as he always had done. He gave thanks to God and asked for his help.

The officials went to Daniel's house and saw him praying.

They went to the king and told him what they'd seen. When the king heard this, he was very upset. He spent the whole day trying to think of a way to save Daniel. But no law signed by the Babylonian king could be overruled.

At last, the king gave orders for Daniel to be thrown into the lions' den. King Darius said to him, "You always serve your God faithfully. So may he save you!"

Then the lions' den was sealed shut with Daniel inside. The king didn't eat anything all night and couldn't sleep. Very early in the morning, he hurried to the lions' den. He called out, "Daniel! You serve the living God. Has he been able to save you from the lions?"

Daniel answered, "My God sent his angel. And his angel shut the mouths of the lions. They haven't hurt me at all because I haven't done anything wrong in God's sight."

The king was filled with joy and ordered that Daniel be taken out of the lions' den. Then the king ordered the court officials who had plotted against Daniel to be thrown in the lions' den. Daniel was safe, there was not a scratch on him, for he trusted in God.

Esther's Request to the King
Esther 3-8

This is Esther. She was a Jewish woman who lived in Persia during the reign of King Xerxes. Esther didn't have a father or mother, so she was adopted by her relative, Mordecai, who worked in the palace of the king. Esther married King Xerxes and became the queen of Persia, but no one knew that she was Jewish. Mordecai told her to keep it a secret.

Haman was the second most powerful man in Persia. Haman hated Mordecai because Mordecai wouldn't bow down to him. So Haman convinced King Xerxes to make an order to kill all Mordecai's people, the Jews.

When Mordecai learned about this, he was so upset that he put on ashes and sackcloth. Mordecai sent a message to Esther telling her to go to the king to ask him to save the Jews. Esther knew that anyone who went to the king without being called could be put to death. But Mordecai said, "Who knows? It's possible that you became queen for such a time as this."

So Esther asked the Jews to fast for three days.
Then she put on her royal robes and went before the king.

King Xerxes was pleased to see Esther and said, "What do you want? I'll give it to you. I'll even give you up to half of my kingdom."

Esther asked the king if he and Haman would come to a banquet that she had prepared for them. The king agreed.

Esther held the banquet, and then asked the king and Haman to come to another banquet the next night. At the second banquet, Esther told the king about the plot against her people. The king was angry and asked, "Who is the man who has dared do such a thing?" Esther said it was Haman, and the king ordered Haman to be killed on that very night.

But the order to kill all the Jews was still in place, and they were still in danger. So Mordecai asked the king to issue a new order so that the Jews could defend themselves. The king did, and the Jews defeated all their enemies. God's people were saved and celebrated their great victory!

Nehemiah Rebuilds the Wall
Nehemiah 1-9

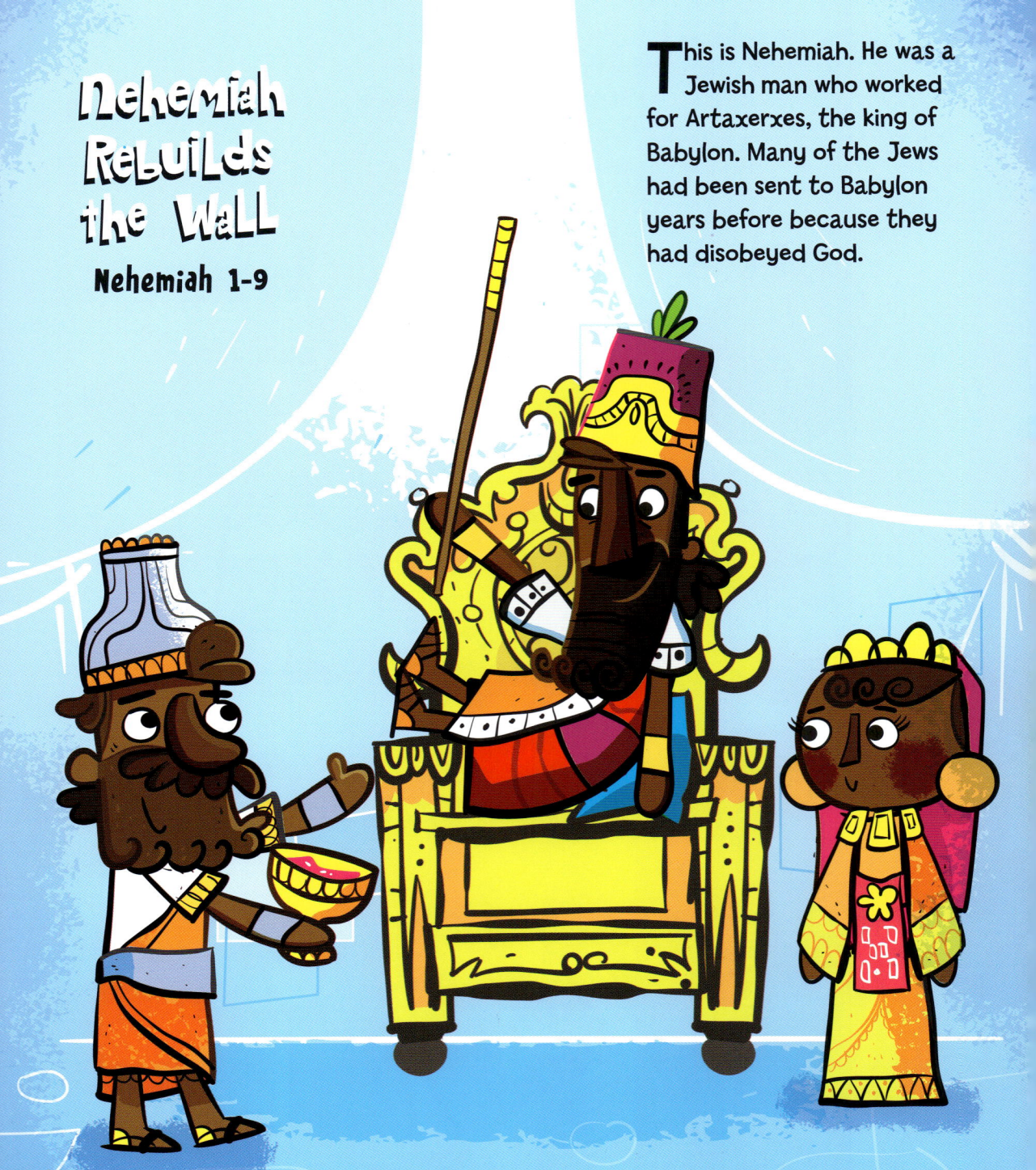

This is Nehemiah. He was a Jewish man who worked for Artaxerxes, the king of Babylon. Many of the Jews had been sent to Babylon years before because they had disobeyed God.

One day Nehemiah heard that the Jews who had returned to Judah were having a hard time. The walls of Jerusalem were broken down, and the gates had been burned.

This made Nehemiah sad. He didn't eat any food for days and prayed to God. He told God he was sorry for the wrong things he and his people had done. He reminded God of his promises and that God had said, "If you obey my commands, I will gather you together again." Nehemiah asked God to give him success as he went to ask the king for help.

Nehemiah then went to do his job for the king. The king asked why Nehemiah was sad, and Nehemiah told him about his people in Judah. Nehemiah prayed and told the king he wanted to rebuild the city of Jerusalem. So the king gave him letters that would help him travel safely to Jerusalem and get the supplies he needed to rebuild the city.

Nehemiah went to Jerusalem and checked out the walls. He went to the people and said, "Come on. Let's rebuild the wall of Jerusalem." The people agreed and started that good work.

Meanwhile, there were some officials from nearby lands who heard Nehemiah was rebuilding the wall. That made them angry, and they made fun of the Jews. But Nehemiah said, "The God of heaven will give us success. We serve him."

Many Jews worked together to rebuild the wall, including the priests, leaders, servants, guards, traders, and women as well. All the people worked with all their hearts.

The officials from other lands planned to fight the Jews. But the Jews prayed to God and put guards on duty day and night. Nehemiah stationed people to defend the city where it was weak. From that day on, half of the people did the work with swords at their sides, and the other half were armed to defend the people working and the city.

Nehemiah reminded them, "Our God will fight for us!"
Every day, they worked from sunrise until the stars came out.

After 52 days, the city wall was finally finished! All of Judah's enemies were afraid because they realized that God had helped finish the work. Jerusalem was large. It had a lot of room. But only a few people lived there. So God gave Nehemiah the idea to gather more people to come and live in Jerusalem now that the wall had been rebuilt, and many people returned. God gathered his people together again.

A teacher of God's law named Ezra came and read the Book of the Law to all the people. The Israelites admitted they had sinned. Then they worshiped God, and promised to follow God's commands.

The

206

New Testament

The Story of Christmas

Matthew 1:18–2:23;
Luke 1:26–38;
2:1-40

Joseph's Woodworking Shop

This is Mary. Mary lived in the town of Nazareth and was engaged to marry a man named Joseph.

One day, God sent the angel Gabriel to Mary. Gabriel told Mary that God was with her and would use her in a special way.

Gabriel said, "Do not be afraid, Mary. God is very pleased with you. You will become pregnant and give birth to a son. You must call him Jesus. The Son of the Most High God will rule forever over his people."

208

Mary asked, "But how can this happen?" Gabriel told Mary that the Holy Spirit would make her pregnant, so that the baby born would be holy and called the Son of God! The angel reminded her that, "What God says will always come true!" So Mary decided to trust God and all that he had planned for her.

When Joseph found out that Mary was pregnant, he thought she had done something wrong. But Joseph was a man of God and decided to end the engagement quietly so no one would think badly of Mary.

While Joseph was thinking about all this, an angel appeared to him in a dream. The angel said, "Joseph, son of David, don't be afraid to make Mary your wife. The baby inside her is from the Holy Spirit. You must give him the name Jesus. He will save his people from their sins." And when Joseph woke up he did as the angel told him to and took Mary as his wife.

After Mary and Joseph were married, and while she was pregnant with Jesus, the ruler of the land, Caesar Augustus, announced that he wanted to make a list of all the people in the land.

So Mary and Joseph traveled from Nazareth to Bethlehem to be counted with Joseph's family.

Nazareth
Israel
Bethlehem

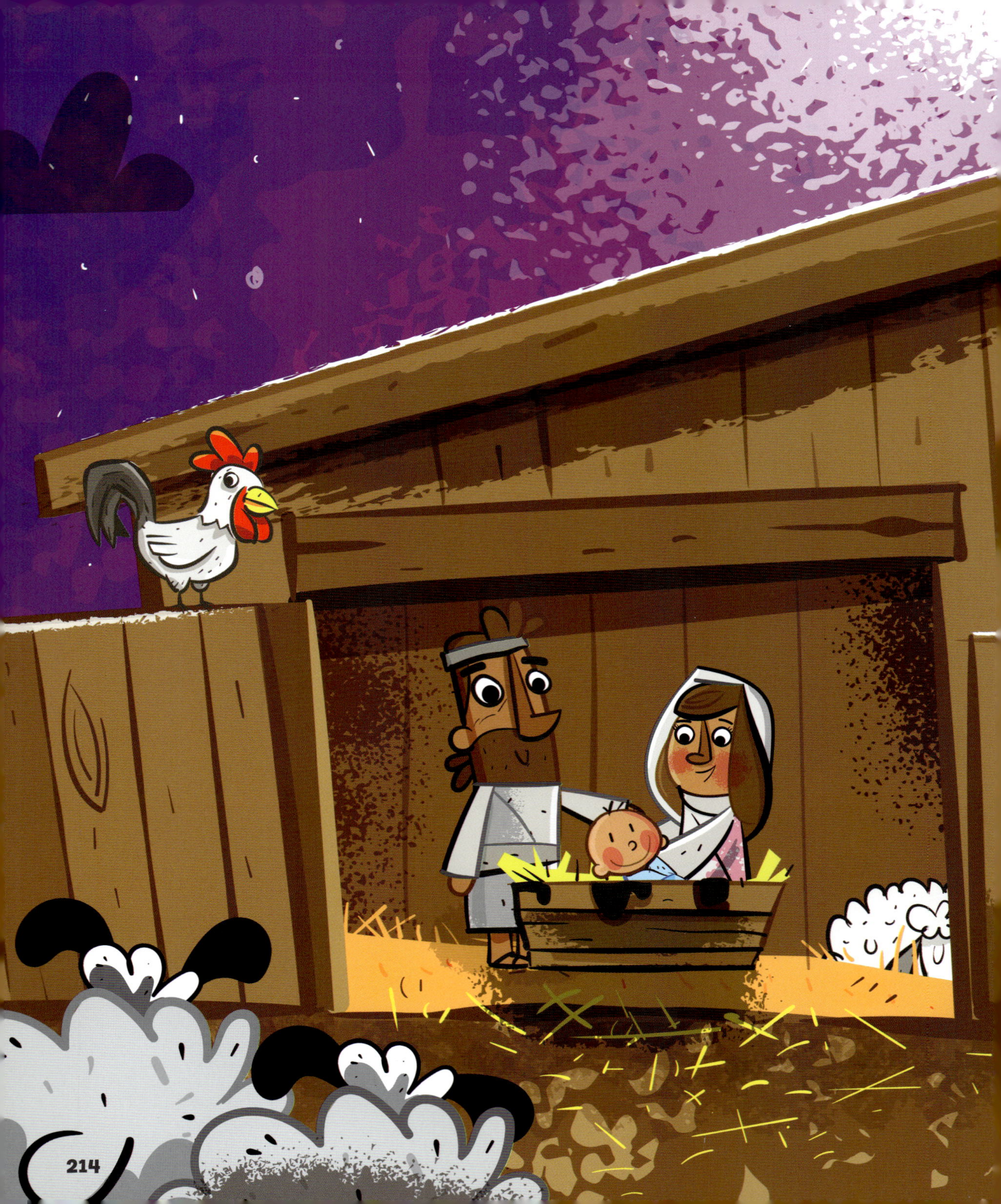

When Mary and Joseph arrived in Bethlehem, they looked for a place to stay. But there was no room for them. While they were there, Jesus was born! Mary wrapped him in large strips of cloth and placed him in a manger.

That night, there were some shepherds in a field taking care of their sheep when an angel appeared to them. God's glory shone all around them! The shepherds were terrified, but the angel said, "Do not be afraid. I bring you good news. It will bring great joy for all the people. Today in the town of David a Savior has been born to you! He is the Messiah, the Lord."

The angel told the shepherds that they would find Jesus wrapped in strips of cloth, laying in a manger.

Then the angel was joined by many other angels, and all of them sang, "Glory to God in the highest heaven! And on earth peace to those whom he favors!"

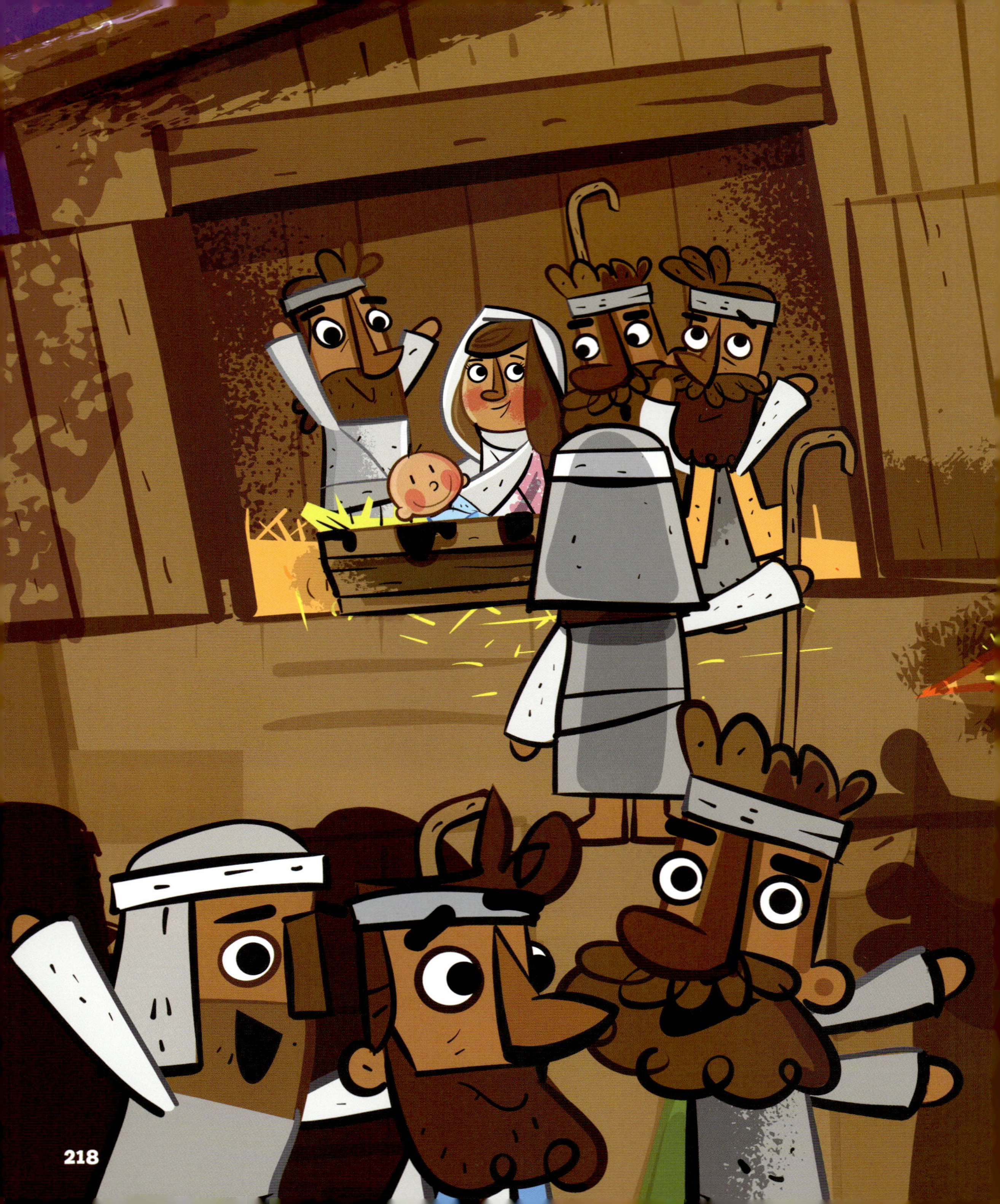

Then the angels went to heaven and the shepherds said to each other, "Let's go to Bethlehem!" So they hurried off and found Mary, Joseph, and the baby Jesus laying in the manger.

After seeing Jesus, the shepherds told everyone what had happened and what the angel had said. All who heard the shepherds' story were amazed. Mary made sure she remembered all these things and thought about them often. The shepherds went back to their sheep and praised God for all they had seen.

The city of Bethlehem, where Jesus had been born, was ruled by a king named Herod. King Herod was in Jerusalem when some wise men from the east arrived asking, "Where is the child who has been born to be king of the Jews? We saw his star when it rose. Now we have come to worship him."

When Herod heard this, he was very upset. He sent the wise men to Bethlehem and said, "As soon as you find him, report it to me. Then I can go and worship him too." But Herod didn't want to worship Jesus. He wanted to get rid of him.

The wise men went on their way to Bethlehem. The star they had seen went ahead of them and stopped over the place where Jesus was. When they saw the star, the wise men were filled with joy!

They went into the house and saw Mary and Jesus. They bowed down and worshiped Jesus. They gave him special gifts fit for the king that he was—gold, frankincense, and myrrh. But God warned them in a dream not to go back to Herod. So they returned to their country on a different road.

Nazareth

Israel

Jerusalem

Bethlehem

Then an angel appeared to Joseph in a dream and said, "Get up!" The angel told Joseph to take his family to Egypt because Herod wanted to kill Jesus.

During the night, Joseph left for Egypt with Jesus and Mary. They stayed in Egypt until Herod was gone and it was safe for them to go home to Israel. When they returned to Israel, the new ruler was Herod's son, so Joseph and his family went to the land of Galilee and lived in the town of Nazareth.

This story showed that many things that had been said about Jesus long ago had come true.

Jesus in the Temple

Luke 2:40-52

This is Jesus. He is the Son of God and the Savior of the world. Jesus grew up in Nazareth and became strong and wise. He was blessed by God's grace.

Every year Jesus' parents went to Jerusalem for the Passover Festival. When Jesus was 12, they went to Jerusalem just like every other year.

After the festival was over, Mary and Joseph were heading back home with a group of people when they realized that Jesus was not with them. They went back to Jerusalem and searched for him for three days.

1
2
3

They finally found him in the temple. Jesus was sitting with the teachers, listening to them and asking them questions. They were all amazed at how much he understood.

Mary said, "Your father and I have been worried about you. We have been looking for you everywhere." But Jesus said, "Why were you looking for me? Didn't you know I had to be in my Father's house?" But his parents didn't understand what he meant.

Jesus went home with them, and he obeyed them. Jesus became wiser and stronger and grew in favor with God and man.

John the Baptist

Matthew 3:1-12; Mark 1:18; Luke 1:5-7, 23-25, 39-44; 3:1-18

This is John the Baptist. John was the son of a Jewish priest named Zechariah and Elizabeth. John's parents were very old when Elizabeth became pregnant with John. Elizabeth's cousin was Mary, Jesus' mother. After the angel told Mary she would become pregnant with the Son of God, she went to visit Elizabeth. When Elizabeth heard Mary's greeting, Elizabeth felt John jump in her belly.

As John grew up his spirit became strong. He lived in the wilderness and ate locusts and honey. He wore clothes made from camel's hair.

John was a messenger of God, and his job was to prepare the way for Jesus.

John preached that people should be baptized to show that they had repented of their sins and turned to God to be forgiven. Great crowds came to John to be baptized.

Many thought that John was the Messiah, the Savior of the world that they were waiting for. But John said, "I baptize you with water. But one who is more powerful than I am will come. I'm not good enough to untie the straps of his sandals. He will baptize you with the Holy Spirit."

Jesus is Baptized

Matthew 3:13-17; Mark 1:9-11; Luke 3:21-22; John 1:29-34

John the Baptist baptized people in the Jordan River. One day, Jesus went to the river to be baptized by John too. But John tried to stop him. John thought Jesus should be baptizing him instead!

But Jesus said, "It is right for us to do this. It carries out God's holy plan."

So John baptized Jesus. As Jesus came out of the water, the heavens opened. Jesus and John saw the Holy Spirit come down on Jesus like a dove.

A voice from heaven said, "This is my Son, and I love him. I am very pleased with him."

And John knew this was God's Chosen One who he had been telling people about, who would take away the sin of the world.

Jesus Changes Water into Wine

John 2:1-11

One day Jesus, his disciples, and his mother, Mary, went to a wedding in Cana. During the party, the wine ran out. So Jesus' mother said to him, "They have no more wine."

Jesus said, "Dear woman, why are you telling me about this? The time for me to show who I really am isn't here yet."

But Mary told the servants, "Do what he tells you."

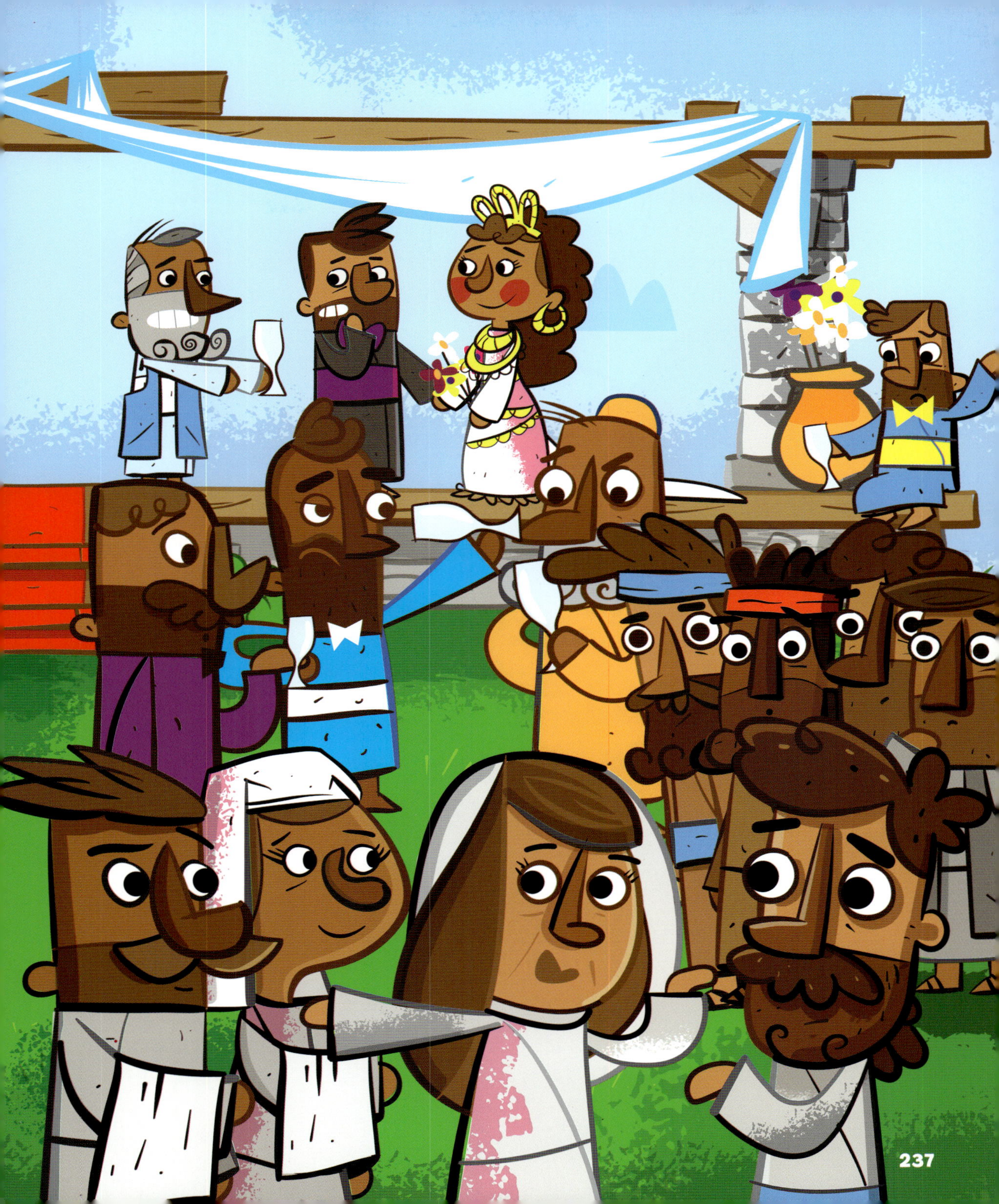

There were six stone jars nearby. Jesus told the servants, "Fill the jars with water." When the jars had been filled, he said, "Now pour some out and take it to the person in charge of the dinner." So the servants did what Jesus told them to.

When the person in charge tasted the water that had been turned to wine he called the groom over. The person in charge didn't know where the wine had come from. He said to the groom, "Everyone brings out the best wine first. They bring out the cheaper wine after the guests have had too much to drink. But you have saved the best until now."

What Jesus did in Cana was the first of his miracles. He showed his glory by doing this, and his disciples believed in him.

Jesus Forgives and Heals a Man Who Could Not Walk

Matthew 9:1-8; Mark 2:1-12; Luke 5:15-26

The news about Jesus had spread all around, so many people wanted to see what he was doing. One day Jesus was in Capernaum teaching God's Word in a house. Soon the house was so full of people there was no room to get in.

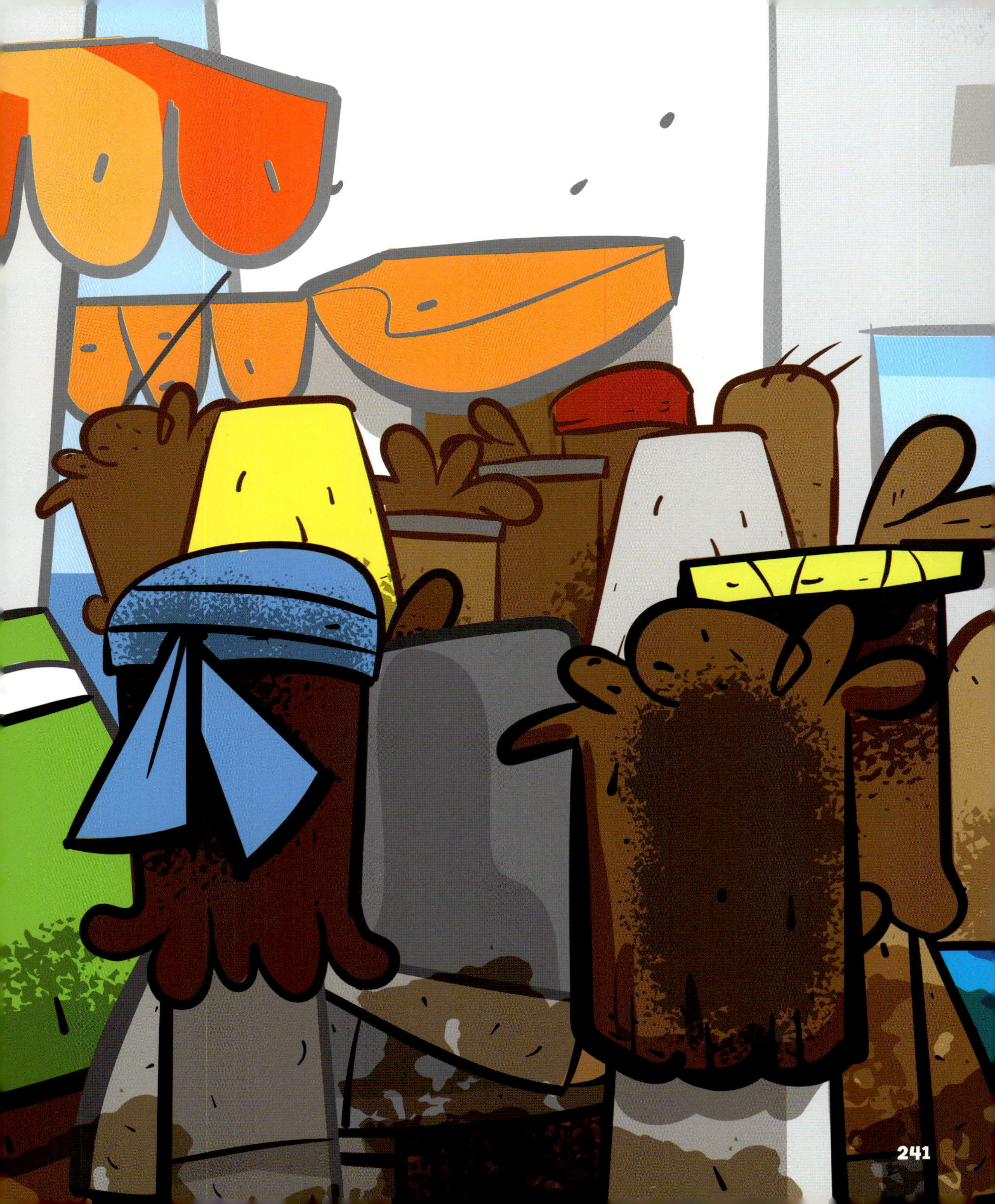

Four men heard that Jesus was in town and that he had the power to heal the sick. They had a friend who could not walk, and they wanted to take him to Jesus. When they got to the house, they couldn't reach Jesus because of the crowd.

So they went to the roof and took off some of the roof tiles to make a hole. Then they lowered their friend down into the middle of the crowd, right in front of Jesus.

Jesus saw their faith. He said to the man, "Son, your sins are forgiven."

There were some Pharisees and teachers of the law in the room, and they did not like what Jesus said. They thought to themselves, "He's saying a very evil thing! Only God can forgive sins!"

Jesus knew what they were thinking and said, "The Son of Man has authority on earth to forgive sins." Then Jesus said to the man who couldn't walk, "Get up. Take your mat and go home."

Right away, the man stood up in front of them. He took his mat and went home, praising God. All the people were amazed as they watched the man walk out through the crowd. They praised God saying, "We have never seen anything like this!"

The Lord's Prayer

Matthew 6:9-13

Jesus said, "This is how you should pray:

'Our Father in heaven,
   may your name be honored.
May your kingdom come.
May what you want to happen be done
   on earth as it is done in heaven.
Give us today our daily bread.
And forgive us our sins,
   just as we also have forgiven those who sin against us.
Keep us from sinning when we are tempted.
   Save us from the evil one.'"

247

The Faith of a Roman Commander

Matthew 8:5-13

Jesus was in Capernaum when a Roman commander came to him and asked for help. The commander's servant couldn't move and was lying in bed with terrible pain. Jesus said, "Shall I come and heal him?"

But the Roman commander said that he wasn't good enough to have Jesus come to his house. He said, "Just say the word and my servant will be healed." When Jesus heard this, he was amazed. Jesus turned to his followers and said, "What I'm about to tell you is true. In Israel I have not found anyone whose faith is so strong."

Then Jesus said to the Roman commander, "Go! It will be done just as you believed it would." And the servant was healed at that moment.

Jesus' Story of the Farmer

Matthew 13:1-9, 18-23; Mark 4:1-20; Luke 8:4-15

One day Jesus went and sat beside the sea. A great crowd gathered around him, so he got in a boat and taught them many things through stories called parables. He told them this story.

"A farmer went out to plant his seed. He scattered the seed on the ground. Some fell on a path. People walked on it, and the birds ate it up. Some seed fell on rocky ground. When it grew, the plants dried up because they had no water. Other seed fell among thorns. The thorns grew up with it and crowded out the plants. Still other seed fell on good soil. It grew up and produced a crop 100 times more than the farmer planted."

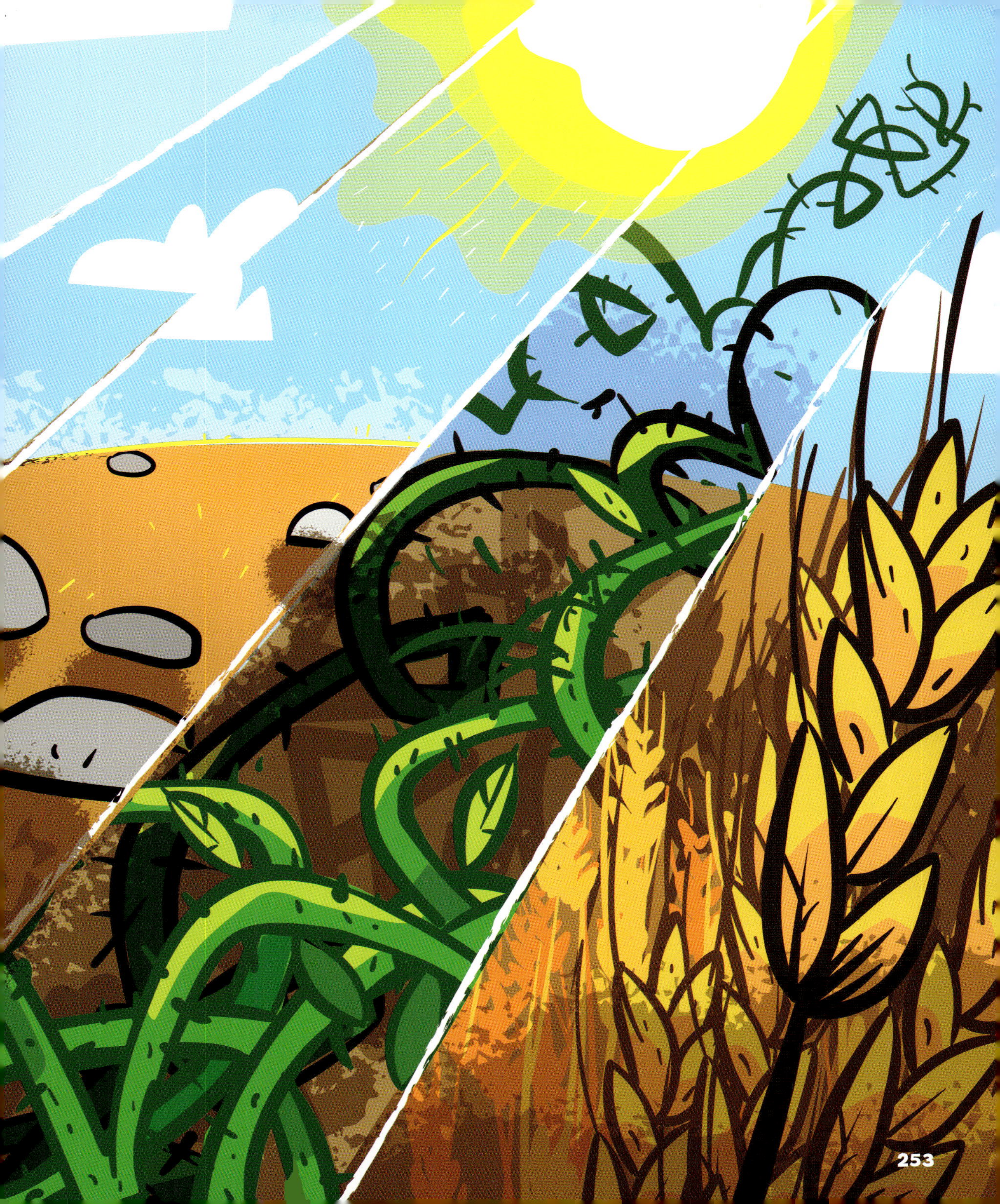

Later, the disciples asked Jesus what the story meant. Jesus said, "The seed is God's message. The seed on the path stands for God's message in the hearts of those who hear. But then the devil comes. He takes away the message from their hearts, so that they may not believe and be saved.

"The seed on rocky ground stands for those who hear the message and receive it with joy. But they have no roots. They believe for a while. But when they are tested, they fall away from the faith. The seed that fell among thorns stands for those who hear the message. But as they go on their way, they are choked by life's worries, riches, and pleasures.

"So they do not reach full growth. But the seed that fell on good soil is like those who hear the message and understand it. They keep it in their hearts. They remain faithful and produce a good crop."

Jesus Calms the Storm

Matthew 8:23-27;
Mark 4:35-41; Luke 8:22-25

One day after preaching to a crowd of people, Jesus said to his disciples, "Let's go over to the other side of the lake." So they got into a boat and left.

As they sailed, Jesus fell asleep. But soon a wild storm came down on the lake. Giant waves crashed over the boat, and it was about to sink. They were in great danger.

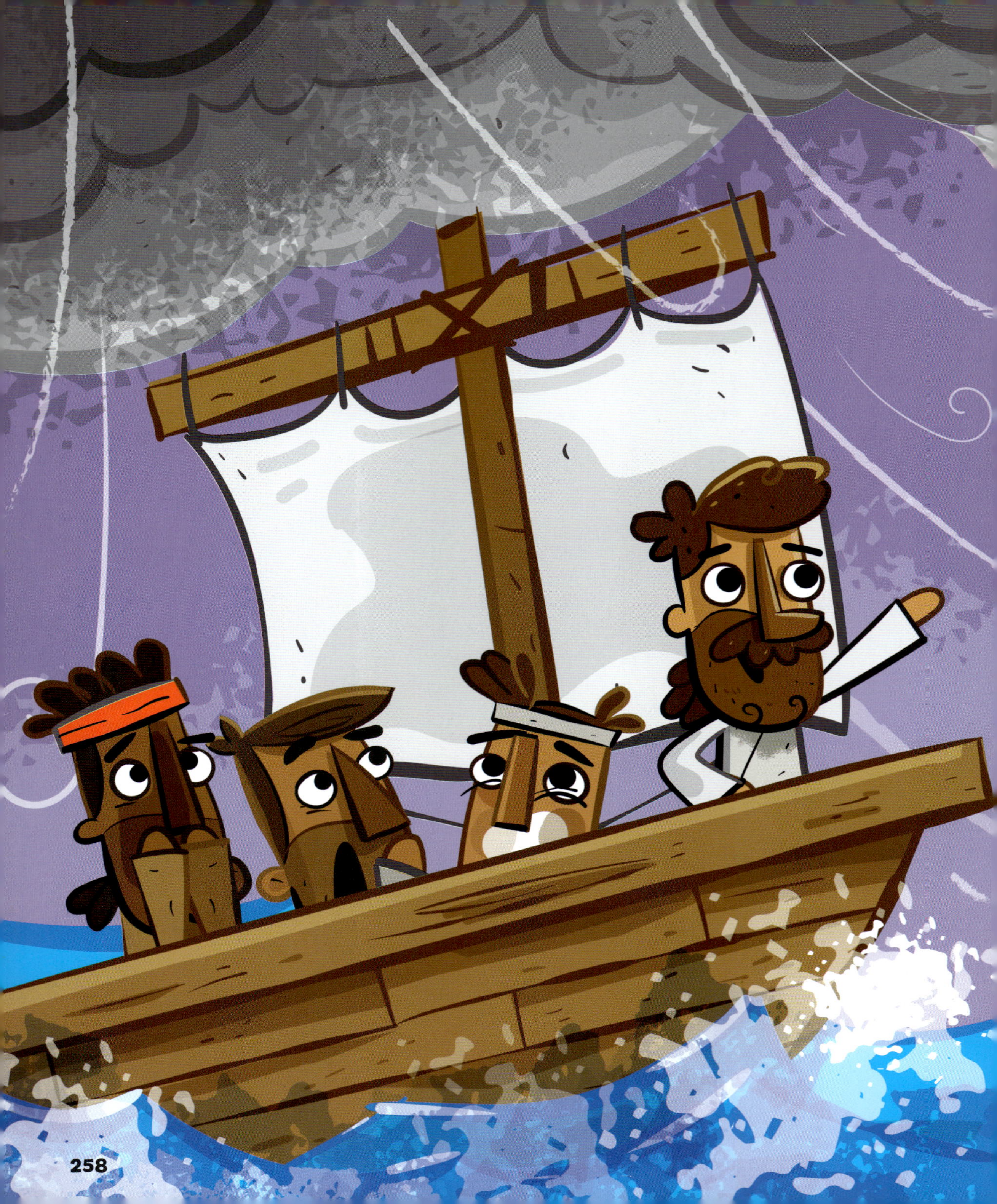

The disciples woke Jesus up, shouting, "Save us! We are going to drown! Don't you care if we drown?" Jesus responded, "Your faith is so small! Why are you afraid?" Then Jesus got up and said to the wind and the waves, "Quiet! Be still!"

As soon as Jesus spoke, the wind stopped. It was completely calm. Then he asked his disciples, "Where is your faith?"

The disciples were terrified and amazed. They asked each other, "Who is this? Even the wind and the waves obey him!"

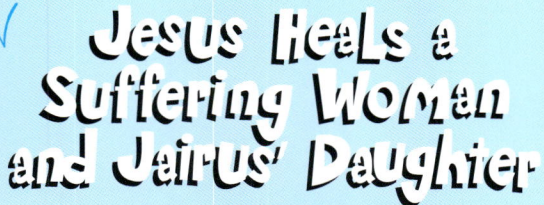

Jesus Heals a Suffering Woman and Jairus' Daughter

Matthew 9:18-26; Mark 5:21-43; Luke 8:40-56

One day a crowd met Jesus as he was getting off a boat. A Jewish leader named Jairus came to Jesus and begged him to come to his home because his 12-year-old daughter was dying.

A woman in the crowd had been sick for 12 years and had spent all her money paying doctors to help her, but she'd only gotten worse. When she heard about Jesus, she thought to herself, "I just need to touch his clothes. Then I will be healed."

So the woman came up behind Jesus and touched his clothes. Right away, the woman was healed!

Jesus felt that healing power had gone out from him, so he asked, "Who touched my clothes?"

Everyone in the crowd said they didn't do it, but Jesus kept looking because he knew someone touched him on purpose.

The woman realized she couldn't stay hidden, so she fell on her knees before Jesus and explained why she had touched him. Jesus said to her, "Dear woman, your faith has healed you. Go in peace. You are free from your suffering."

As this was happening, a messenger arrived from Jairus' house and told him his daughter was dead so there was no need to trouble Jesus anymore.

But when Jesus heard what happened, he said to Jairus, "Don't be afraid. Just believe. She will be healed."

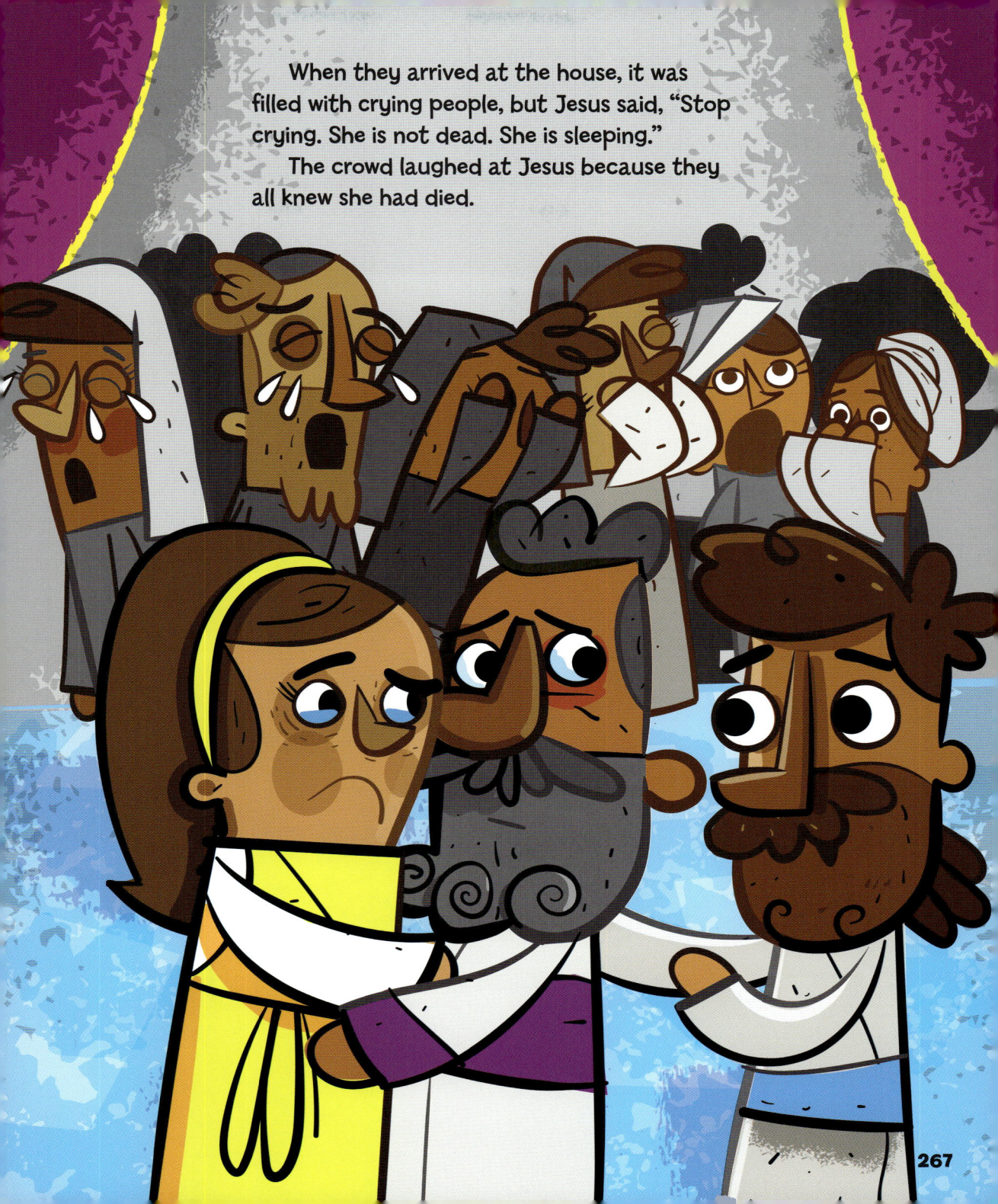

When they arrived at the house, it was filled with crying people, but Jesus said, "Stop crying. She is not dead. She is sleeping."

The crowd laughed at Jesus because they all knew she had died.

Jesus made everyone leave except Peter, James, John, and the girl's parents. Then Jesus took the girl by the hand and said in a loud voice, "Little girl, get up!"

And right away, the girl stood up and started walking around! Her parents were amazed, but Jesus insisted that they not tell anyone what had happened. But news still spread all throughout the region of the miracle Jesus had done.

Jesus Feeds the 5,000

Matthew 14:13-21;
Mark 6:30-44;
Luke 9:10-17;
John 6:1-13

One day a crowd gathered around Jesus. These crowds followed Jesus wherever he went because they saw the amazing miracles he did. There were 5,000 men and many more women and children. Jesus said to his disciple, Philip, "Where can we buy bread for these people to eat?"

Jesus already knew what he was going to do. He only asked this to test Philip. Philip answered him, "Even if we worked for months, we wouldn't have enough money to feed them!"

Then Andrew spoke up. "Here is a boy with five small loaves of barley bread. He also has two small fish. But how far will that go in such a large crowd?"

Jesus said, "Have the people sit down."

Then Jesus took the loaves, gave thanks to God, and gave the bread to the people. Afterward he did the same with the fish.

They all ate as much as they wanted. After everyone was full, Jesus told his disciples, "Gather the leftover pieces. Don't waste anything."

So they gathered the leftovers and filled 12 baskets with leftover food from the five barley loaves and two fish.

Jesus Walks on Water

Matthew 14:22-33; Mark 6:45-52; John 6:16-21

After Jesus had done a great miracle in front of a crowd of people, he sent the disciples in a boat across the Sea of Galilee. Jesus stayed and sent the people home. Then he went up a mountainside by himself to pray.

Meanwhile, the disciples were having trouble on the water. A strong wind had risen, and they were fighting heavy waves. Before dawn, Jesus came toward them, walking on the water. When the disciples saw him walking on the water, they were terrified. They cried, "It's a ghost!" But Jesus said, "Be brave! It is I. Don't be afraid."

Then Peter called to him, "Lord, is it you? If it is, tell me to come to you on the water."

Jesus said, "Come."

So Peter got out of the boat. He walked on the water toward Jesus.

But when Peter saw the strong wind, he was afraid. He began to sink. He shouted, "Lord! Save me!"

Right away, Jesus reached out and grabbed his hand. Jesus said, "Your faith is so small. Why did you doubt me?"

When they climbed into the boat, the wind stopped. Then the disciples worshiped him and said, "You really are the Son of God!"

Jesus' Story of the Good Samaritan

Luke 10:25-37

One day a religious expert tried to test Jesus by asking him, "Teacher, what should I do to receive eternal life?"

Jesus replied, "What is written in the Law?"

The man answered, "'Love the Lord your God with all your heart and with all your soul. Love him with all your strength and with all your mind.' And, 'Love your neighbor as you love yourself.'"

Jesus said he was right and then said, "Do that, and you will live!"

The man then asked, "Who is my neighbor?"

Jesus answered with a story. "A Jewish man was going down from Jerusalem to Jericho. Robbers attacked him. They stripped off his clothes and beat him. Then they went away, leaving him almost dead.

"A priest happened to be going down that same road. When he saw the man, he passed by on the other side. A Levite also came by. When he saw the man, he passed by on the other side too.

"But a Samaritan came to the place where the man was. When he saw the man, he felt sorry for him. He went to him, poured olive oil and wine on his wounds, and bandaged them.

"Then he put the man on his own donkey. He brought him to an inn and took care of him. The next day he took out two silver coins. He gave them to the owner of the inn. 'Take care of him,' he said. 'When I return, I will pay you back for any extra expense you may have.'"

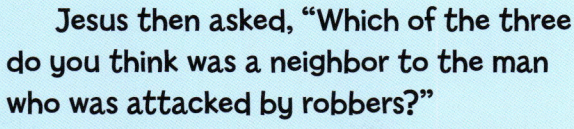

Jesus then asked, "Which of the three do you think was a neighbor to the man who was attacked by robbers?"

The religious expert replied, "The one who had mercy on him."

Then Jesus said, "Go and do as he did."

Jesus Visits Mary and Martha

Luke 10:38-42

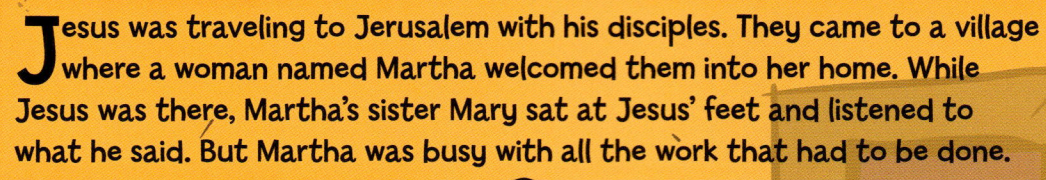

Jesus was traveling to Jerusalem with his disciples. They came to a village where a woman named Martha welcomed them into her home. While Jesus was there, Martha's sister Mary sat at Jesus' feet and listened to what he said. But Martha was busy with all the work that had to be done.

Martha came to Jesus and said, "Lord, my sister has left me to do the work by myself. Don't you care? Tell her to help me!"

But Jesus said to her, "Martha, you are worried and upset about so many things. But only one thing is needed. Mary has chosen what is better. And it will not be taken away from her."

Jesus' Story of the Great Banquet

Matthew 22:1-14; Luke 14:12-24

One day Jesus went to eat at the house of a Pharisee. He said to the Pharisee, "When you host a dinner, do not invite your friends, family, or rich neighbors. For they will invite you back, and that will be your only reward. Instead, invite the poor and those who have trouble seeing and walking. Then God will reward you for inviting those who could not repay you."

When a man at the table heard what Jesus said, he said to Jesus, "Blessed is the one who will eat at the feast in God's kingdom."

Jesus replied with a story: "A man was preparing a great banquet and invited many guests. Then the day of the banquet arrived. He sent his servant to those who had been invited.

"The servant told them, 'Come. Everything is ready now.' But they all began to make excuses. The first one said, 'I have just bought a field. I have to go and look at it. Please excuse me.' Another said, 'I have just bought five pairs of oxen. I'm on my way to try them out. Please excuse me.' Still another said, 'I just got married, so I can't come.'

"The servant came back and reported this to his master. Then the owner of the house became angry. He ordered his servant, 'Go out quickly into the streets. Bring in those who are poor and those who can't see or walk, anyone you can find. I want my house to be full.'

"The servant did so, until the hall was filled with guests. Not one of the people who were invited got a taste of the banquet. For though many are invited, only a few are chosen."

Jesus' Story of the Lost Sheep

Matthew 18:12-14;
Luke 15:1-7

Jesus taught everyone about God's love. All kinds of people would come to hear Jesus speak, including people who made wrong choices. This made the Pharisees and Jewish leaders angry. They didn't think Jesus should be around these kinds of people.

So Jesus told them this story:

"Suppose a man owns 100 sheep and one of them wanders away.

"Won't he leave the 99 others and go to search for the one that is lost until he finds it? When he finds it, he will joyfully put it on his shoulders and go home. Then he will call his friends and neighbors together. He will say, 'Celebrate with me. I have found my lost sheep.'

"I tell you, it will be the same in heaven. There will be great joy when one sinner turns away from sin. Yes, there will be more joy than for 99 godly people who do not need to turn away from their sins. For your Father in heaven does not want any of these little children to be lost."

Jesus' Story of the Lost Son

Luke 15:11-32

One day Jesus told a story about God's love. "There was a man who had two sons. The younger son asked his father to give him his share of the family property. So the father divided his property between his two sons.

Then the younger son packed up all he had and left for a country far away.

"There he wasted his money on wild living, until he'd spent everything his father had given him.

Then the whole country ran low on food, and the younger son had to take a job feeding pigs. He was so hungry, he wanted to eat the food the pigs were eating. But no one gave him anything.

Then he said, 'My father's servants have more than enough food! But here I am dying from hunger. I will get up and go back to my father.'

"So he got up and went to his father to apologize for what he had done. While the son was still a long way off, his father saw him. He was filled with tender love for his son.

"He ran to him. He threw his arms around him and kissed him.
 The son said to him, 'Father, I have sinned against heaven and against you. I am no longer fit to be called your son.'
 But the father said to his servants, 'Quick! Bring the best robe and put it on him. Put a ring on his finger and sandals on his feet. Let's have a feast and celebrate. This son of mine was lost. And now he is found.' So they began to celebrate.

"The older son was in the field. When he came near the house, he heard music and dancing, so he asked a servant what was going on. The servant told him, 'Your father has killed the fattest calf because your brother is back safe and sound.'

"The older brother became angry and refused to go in. So his father went out and begged him. He answered, 'All these years I've worked for you and obeyed your orders. You never gave me even a young goat so I could celebrate with my friends. But this son of yours wasted your money. Now he comes home. And for him you kill the fattest calf!'

"The father said, 'My son, you are always with me. Everything I have is yours. But we had to celebrate and be glad. This brother of yours was dead. And now he is alive again. He was lost. And now he is found.'"

The Thankful Man

Luke 17:11-19

Leprosy was a skin disease that gave people sores on their bodies. It was very contagious, so people with leprosy were sent away from where they lived. In Jesus' time, these people were called unclean, and no one wanted to be close to them.

One day, ten men who had leprosy met Jesus as he was on his way to Jerusalem. They called out, "Jesus! Master! Have pity on us!"

Jesus saw them and said, "Go. Show yourselves to the priests." While they were on their way, they realized they were healed. Their leprosy was gone! Then one of the men, who was a Samaritan, ran back to Jesus. He praised God and threw himself at Jesus' feet, thanking him for what he had done.

Jesus asked, "Weren't all ten healed? Where are the other nine? Didn't anyone else return and give praise to God?"

Then Jesus said to the man, "Get up and go. Your faith has healed you." The man was healed because he had faith and he was thankful for what Jesus had done for him.

Jesus and the Children

Matthew 19:13-15;
Mark 10:13-16;
Luke 18:15-17

One day some parents brought their children to Jesus so he could bless them. But the disciples told the parents to stop.

When Jesus saw what was happening, he was angry. He said to his disciples, "Let the little children come to me. Don't keep them away. God's kingdom belongs to people like them. What I'm about to tell you is true. Anyone who will not receive God's kingdom like a little child will never enter it."

Then he took the children in his arms and blessed them.

307

Zacchaeus
Luke 19:1-10

This is Zacchaeus, who was a tax collector in Jericho and very rich. A lot of people hated tax collectors because they thought they were liars and cheaters. Zacchaeus heard that Jesus was passing through town. Zacchaeus wanted to see Jesus, but he was too short to see above the crowd.

So he ran ahead to a place where he knew Jesus would come. He climbed a sycamore tree so he could see Jesus. When Jesus came by, he looked up and saw Zacchaeus in the tree. He said to him, "Zacchaeus, come down at once. I must stay at your house today."

Zacchaeus came down and welcomed Jesus gladly. All the people saw this and began to complain, "Jesus has gone to be the guest of a sinner."

But Zacchaeus said to Jesus, "I will give half of my money to the poor. If I have cheated anyone, I will pay that person back four times more!"

Jesus said, "Today salvation has come to your house. The Son of Man came to look for the lost and save them."

Jesus Raises Lazarus from the Dead

John 11:1-44

Jesus had a friend named Lazarus. One day, Lazarus' sisters, Mary and Martha, sent a message to Jesus telling him, "Lord, your dear friend is very sick."

But when Jesus heard about it he said, "This sickness will not end in death. No, it is for God's glory." Jesus loved Martha, Mary, and Lazarus, but he stayed where he was for the next two days. Then he said to his disciples, "Let us go back to Judea. Our friend Lazarus has fallen asleep. I am going to wake him up."

The disciples thought Jesus meant Lazarus was simply sleeping. So Jesus told them plainly, "Lazarus is dead. For your benefit, I am glad I was not there. Now you will believe. But let us go to him."

By the time they arrived, Lazarus had already been in the tomb for four days. Many people had come to be with Mary and Martha because their brother had died.

Martha said to Jesus, "Lord, I wish you had been here! Then my brother would not have died. But I know that even now God will give you anything you ask for."

Jesus told her, "Your brother will rise again."

Martha answered, "Yes, I know he will rise again on the last day."

Jesus told her, "I am the resurrection and the life. Anyone who believes in me will live, even if they die. And whoever lives by believing in me will never die. Do you believe this?"

Martha said, "Yes, Lord. I believe that you are the Messiah, the Son of God. I believe that you are the one who is supposed to come into the world."

Then she went to Mary and told her, "The Teacher is here." So Mary ran quickly to Jesus, followed by the people who were with her.

When Mary saw Jesus, she fell at his feet and said, "Lord, I wish you had been here! Then my brother would not have died."

When Jesus saw her crying and saw the other people crying with her, his spirit became very sad, and he was troubled. "Where have you put him?" Jesus asked.

They led him to the tomb, and Jesus wept. The people who were standing nearby said, "See how much he loved him!" But some said, "He opened the eyes of the blind man. Couldn't he have kept this man from dying?"

Jesus was still sad as he arrived at the tomb. Jesus said, "Take away the stone."

Martha said, "But Lord, by this time there is a bad smell. Lazarus has been in the tomb for four days."

Jesus said, "Didn't I tell you that if you believe, you will see God's glory?" So they took away the stone. Then Jesus said, "Father, I thank you for hearing me. I know that you always hear me. But I said this for the benefit of the people standing here. So they will believe you sent me."

Then Jesus called in a loud voice, "Lazarus, come out!" And Lazarus came out, with his hands, feet, and head still wrapped in strips of linen. Jesus told them, "Unwrap him and let him go!"

And many of the people who were there believed in Jesus, for he had raised Lazarus from the dead.

Jesus Comes to Jerusalem as King

Matthew 21:1-11;
Mark 11:1-11;
Luke 19:28-44;
John 12:12-19

Jesus and his disciples were going to Jerusalem to celebrate the Passover. They stopped in a town on the way, and Jesus told two of his disciples to go ahead of them and find a donkey that no one had ever ridden. He told them to untie it and bring it to him.

So the disciples did what Jesus said and brought him the donkey. A long time ago, before Jesus was even born, God had said the Savior would come to Israel riding a donkey, and now Jesus was doing just as God had said.

The news that Jesus was coming to Jerusalem swept through the city. Many heard about all the amazing things he had done, so they cut palm branches and ran to see him. The Pharisees and religious rulers realized that there was nothing they could do, for everyone was going to see Jesus.

Jesus rode into the city of Jerusalem, and the crowds spread their coats on the road ahead of him. His followers began to shout and sing praises to God for all the wonderful miracles they had seen.

The Pharisees were upset. They said to Jesus, "Tell the people to stop!" But Jesus said, "If they keep quiet, the stones along the road would burst into cheers!"

So the people kept on singing, "Blessings on the King who comes in the name of the Lord! Praise God in highest heaven!"

The entire city of Jerusalem was in an uproar as he entered, asking "Who is this?"

And the crowds replied, "It's Jesus!" And Jesus rode the donkey through the streets of Jerusalem to the temple in a triumphal entry, just as God said he would many years before.

Jesus' Story of the Two Sons

Matthew 21:28-32

Jesus was teaching in the temple in Jerusalem when the Pharisees and religious leaders came up to him. They challenged his authority, and Jesus said, "What do you think about this?

"A man had two sons. He went to the first and said, 'Son, go and work today in the vineyard.'

'I will not,' the son answered. But later he changed his mind and went.

Then the father went to the other son. He said the same thing. The son answered, 'I will, sir.' But he did not go.

"Which of the two sons did what his father wanted?"
"The first," they answered.
Then Jesus explained what the story meant.

Jesus told the Pharisees that sinners and tax collectors would get into the kingdom of God before they did, because the sinners had repented. But the Pharisees and religious leaders didn't believe and follow God's message.

When the Pharisees heard this, they wanted to arrest Jesus. But they were afraid to because the crowds listened to Jesus and believed in him.

The Widow's Offering

Mark 12:41-44; Luke 21:1-4

Jesus was in the temple teaching people and answering questions. He sat down near the place where people would bring their offerings as gifts to God.

He watched as the crowds dropped in their money. He saw rich people drop in lots of money, and then he saw a poor widow come to the offering box. She dropped in two small coins.

Jesus called his disciples to him and said, "What I'm about to tell you is true. That poor widow has put more into the offering box than all the others. They all gave a lot because they are rich. But she gave even though she is poor. She put in everything she had. That was all she had to live on."

The Last Supper

Matthew 26:17-30; Mark 14:12-26; Luke 22:7-23; John 13:18-30

Jesus and his disciples were in Jerusalem to celebrate Passover, a Jewish festival that had been celebrated since the time of Moses, when God brought his people out of Egypt. When it was time to eat the Passover meal, the disciples asked him where they should go.

Jesus said, "Go into the city. A man carrying a jar of water will meet you. Follow him. He will enter a house. Say to its owner, 'The Teacher asks, "Where is my guest room? Where can I eat the Passover meal with my disciples?"' He will show you a large upstairs room with furniture already in it. Prepare for us to eat there." The disciples found everything to be just as Jesus had told them.

Later that evening, Jesus arrived with the twelve disciples. They sat down to eat. Jesus said, "One of you who is eating with me will hand me over to my enemies." He told them that things were supposed to happen this way, but that great sadness would come to the one who betrayed him.

The disciples were very sad and upset. They each asked, "Surely you don't mean me?"

Judas asked Jesus, "Surely you don't mean me, Teacher, do you?"

And Jesus said, "You have said so."

One of the disciples asked Jesus, "Lord, who is it?" Jesus said it was the one who he would give the bread to. He gave the bread to Judas, and Jesus said, "Do quickly what you are going to do." None of the others at the table understood what Jesus meant. Judas left at once to betray Jesus.

As they were eating, Jesus took some bread and gave thanks. He broke it and handed it to the disciples. He said, "Take this and eat it. This is my body." Jesus told them to do this to help remember him.

Then he took a cup of wine and gave thanks to God for it. He handed it to his disciples and said, "All of you drink from it. This is my blood of the covenant. It is poured out to forgive the sins of many people." Jesus comforted and encouraged the disciples. Then they all sang, praising God together.

Jesus Washes His Disciples' Feet
John 13:1-17

While Jesus and his disciples were gathered for their Last Supper together, Jesus got up from the table, took off his outer clothes, and began to wash the disciples' feet. Jesus loved his disciples, and he knew the time was coming for him to leave them and return to heaven.

When Jesus came to Peter, Peter said, "Lord, are you going to wash my feet?"

Jesus said, "You don't realize now what I am doing. But later you will understand."

Peter said, "You will never wash my feet!"

But Jesus then told him that unless he washed his feet, Peter would not belong to him. So Peter said, "Lord not just my feet! Wash my hands and head too!"

But Jesus told him that he just needed to wash his feet for Peter to become clean.

So Jesus finished washing their feet and said that the disciples should do to others as he had done for them. He told them to follow the example that he set for them, to serve each other and not think of themselves as greater than anyone else. Then God would bless them for doing as Jesus had taught them.

The Story of Easter

Matthew 26:36-28:8;
Mark 14:43-16:19;
Luke 23:26-24:10;
John 3:16, 18-19

While Jesus was on earth, he taught everyone about God's love and performed many miracles, like healing people, calming storms, and raising people from the dead.

The Jewish leaders and teachers did not like what Jesus was doing, or how he said he was the Son of God, so they made a plan to arrest him to get rid of him once and for all.

Judas, one of Jesus' disciples, agreed to betray Jesus and give him over to the religious leaders for some money.
Jesus was in a garden praying, and Judas showed the men who Jesus was.

Jesus was arrested and brought before the high council of the religious leaders. They asked him if he was the Messiah, the Son of God.

Jesus said, "I am." The council was furious, and they shouted that Jesus was guilty and that he must die.

So they took Jesus before the Roman ruler Pilate, and he heard the charges against Jesus. Pilate didn't think that Jesus had done anything wrong, so he said he would punish Jesus and then release him.

But the crowd kept screaming louder and louder, "Crucify him!" Because of the pressure from the crowd, Pilate turned Jesus over to the Roman soldiers to be crucified.

Jesus was hurt and spit on. His clothes were taken from him, and a crown made out of thorns was put on his head. He was badly beaten, and the guards mocked him saying, "We honor you, king of the Jews!" And then Jesus was forced to carry his cross to the place where he would be crucified. On the way, the soldiers had a man who was passing by, named Simon, carry the cross for Jesus.

KING OF THE JEWS

Once Jesus made it to the place where he would be crucified, called "The Skull," the soldiers around him nailed him to the cross and waited for him to die. While Jesus was hanging on the cross, many people shouted to him, "Come down from the cross, if you are the Son of God!" But Jesus knew that he had to die to forgive people of their sins.

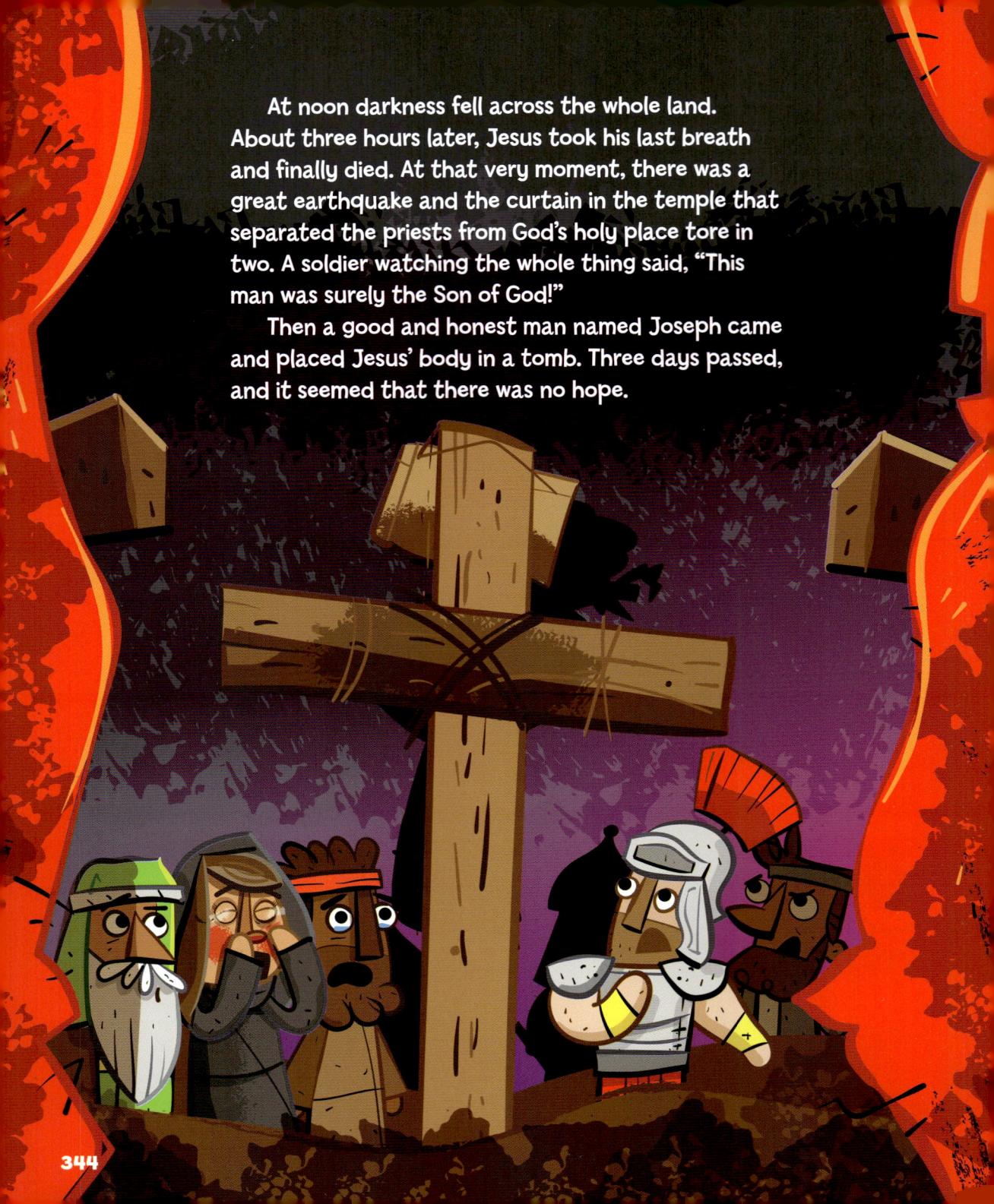

At noon darkness fell across the whole land. About three hours later, Jesus took his last breath and finally died. At that very moment, there was a great earthquake and the curtain in the temple that separated the priests from God's holy place tore in two. A soldier watching the whole thing said, "This man was surely the Son of God!"

Then a good and honest man named Joseph came and placed Jesus' body in a tomb. Three days passed, and it seemed that there was no hope.

But very early on Sunday morning some women who cared for Jesus went to go visit his body. But the huge stone in front of his tomb had been rolled away, and Jesus was no longer inside. The tomb was empty!

An angel, who was sitting on the stone, said to them, "Don't be afraid! He is not here, he is risen!" At this, the women remembered that Jesus had told them he would rise again on the third day. They ran to go tell the disciples what they had seen and heard.

For the next 40 days, Jesus appeared to his disciples and many others and showed them that he was alive and well. He explained that his death and resurrection was the only way everyone's sins could be forgiven, so they could be with God forever. For God so loved the world that he gave his one and only Son. Anyone who believes in him will not die but will have eternal life.

Jesus Appears to Thomas

John 20:24-31

Jesus appeared to his disciples to show them that he was alive. One of the twelve disciples, Thomas, was not with the others when Jesus came. Later, the disciples told Thomas, "We have seen the Lord!"

But Thomas said, "First I must see the nail marks in his hands. I must put my finger where the nails were. I must put my hand into his side. Only then will I believe."

A week later the disciples were together again, and this time Thomas was with them. The doors were locked. Suddenly Jesus came in and stood among them. Jesus said to Thomas, "Put your finger here. See my hands. Reach out your hand and put it into my side. Stop doubting and believe."

Thomas said, "My Lord and my God!"

Then Jesus told him, "Because you have seen me, you have believed. Blessed are those who have not seen me but still have believed."

Jesus Forgives Peter

Matthew 26:31-75;
Mark 14:27-72;
Luke 22:54-62;
John 18:15-27;
21:15-17

This is Peter. Peter was a fisherman and a disciple of Jesus. Before Jesus was taken to die on the cross, he had one final meal with his friends. Jesus told his disciples it was time for him to leave them. Peter said that he would follow Jesus even to his death. But Jesus said, "Before the rooster crows, you will say three times that you don't know me!"

But Peter promised he would never say he didn't know Jesus, as did the other disciples.

Later that night, after Jesus was arrested, Peter and another disciple followed Jesus and his captors to the house of the high priest.

Two servant girls noticed Peter, and both said that he was with Jesus. Both times, Peter said he was not and even said, "I don't know the man!"

Then a man said, "You must have been with Jesus, because you're from Galilee."

But Peter said, "I don't know what you're talking about!" And at that very moment, Peter heard the rooster crow. Jesus turned and looked at Peter. Peter remembered that Jesus had known this would happen, and Peter left that place crying.

Sometime later, after Jesus had died and risen again, Peter and some of the disciples were out fishing. They didn't catch a single fish all night. Early in the morning, Jesus stood on the shore. But the disciples did not realize that it was Jesus.

He called out to them, "Friends, don't you have any fish?"

The disciples said, "No."

Jesus told them to throw their nets to the right of the boat.

So they did, and they couldn't bring in the net because there were too many fish in it! Then one of the disciples said, "It's the Lord!"

So Peter jumped in the water and swam to Jesus.

When the disciples got to the shore, Jesus said, "Come and have breakfast." When they were done eating, Jesus asked Peter three times, "Do you love me?"

Each time Peter said, "You know I love you." And each time Jesus told Peter to feed his lambs and take care of his sheep.

So Peter went on to feed Jesus' sheep by helping to start the church and by writing letters that would become books of the Bible. And even though he had denied knowing Jesus, he was forgiven and many came to know the love and forgiveness of Jesus through Peter.

Jesus Goes to Heaven

Matthew 28:18-20;
Mark 16:15-20;
Luke 24:49-53; Acts 1:6-11

After Jesus' resurrection, he spent 40 days with the disciples and appeared to many people. He told them that he had died so they could be forgiven and be with God forever. Jesus also told them that he would send the Holy Spirit, just as God had promised, to be their helper.

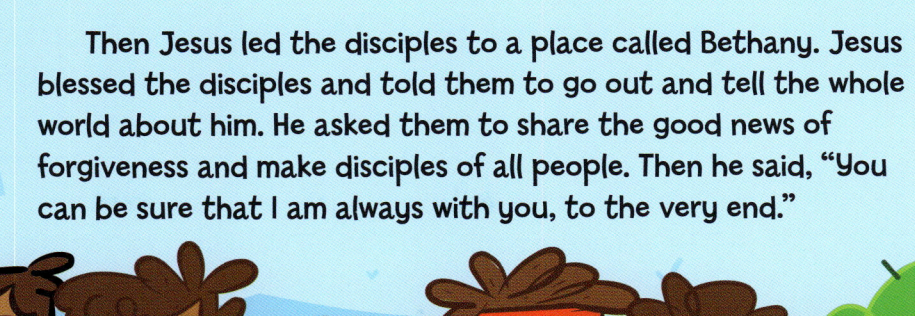

Then Jesus led the disciples to a place called Bethany. Jesus blessed the disciples and told them to go out and tell the whole world about him. He asked them to share the good news of forgiveness and make disciples of all people. Then he said, "You can be sure that I am always with you, to the very end."

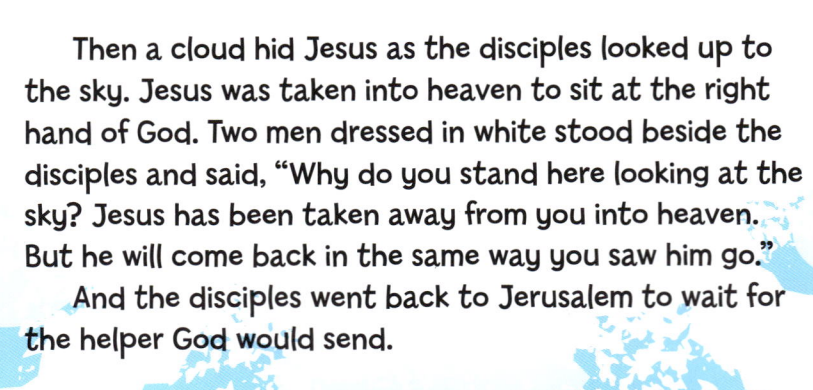

Then a cloud hid Jesus as the disciples looked up to the sky. Jesus was taken into heaven to sit at the right hand of God. Two men dressed in white stood beside the disciples and said, "Why do you stand here looking at the sky? Jesus has been taken away from you into heaven. But he will come back in the same way you saw him go."

And the disciples went back to Jerusalem to wait for the helper God would send.

The Holy Spirit Comes at Pentecost
Acts 2

These are the apostles. They were Jesus' disciples during his time on earth. After Jesus went to heaven, the apostles stayed in Jerusalem, waiting for God to send the gift that Jesus had promised.

One day all the believers were together when the sound of a mighty wind came down from heaven, and something that looked like a flame appeared and rested on each of them. Everyone was filled with the Holy Spirit. The Holy Spirit gave them the ability to speak in languages they hadn't known before.

At that time there were godly Jews from every country staying in Jerusalem. When they heard the loud noise, they came running to see what it was. When they saw the believers speaking in their own languages, they were shocked and amazed!

Then Peter stood up and addressed the crowd. He told them about how Jesus was crucified but then raised to life again just as God had said he would be. He told them Jesus was now in heaven and that God had given the Holy Spirit to them as he had promised.

Peter's words changed what the people thought and felt, and they asked, "What should we do?"

Peter told them, "All of you must turn away from your sins and be baptized in the name of Jesus Christ for the forgiveness of your sins. And you will receive the gift of the Holy Spirit." Peter continued to preach to the crowd for a long time, and three thousand people were baptized and added to the church that day.

Then all the believers listened to the apostles' teaching and practiced what they taught. Everyone was amazed at what God was doing and at the wonders and signs the apostles did. All the believers met together in one place and shared everything they had. They helped those in need, worshiped together at the temple every day, met in homes for communion, and shared their meals with great joy, all while praising God and enjoying each other's company. And every day God added to their group those who were being saved.

Peter Heals a Man Who Could Not Walk
Acts 3

Peter was one of the apostles. Peter told people about Jesus. One day Peter and John were going to the temple to pray. As they were about to enter, a man who couldn't walk was carried in and placed beside the temple gate, so he could beg from the people going in. When the man saw Peter and John, he asked them for some money.

Peter said, "Look at us." The man looked up at them, thinking that they would give him some money. But Peter said, "I don't have any silver or gold. But I'll give you what I do have. In the name of Jesus Christ of Nazareth, get up and walk."

Then Peter took the man by the hand and helped him up. As he did, the man's feet and ankles became strong. He jumped to his feet and began to walk! Then walking, jumping, and praising God, he went into the temple with them.

All the people saw him walking and heard him praising God. When they realized this was the man who couldn't walk who had been sitting outside the gate, they were filled with wonder!

Peter asked the people, "Why does this surprise you? Why do you stare at us? It's not as if we've made this man walk by our own power." He reminded them that it was God's power that healed the man and encouraged all of them to turn from their sins and follow God with their whole hearts.

Philip and the Man from Ethiopia

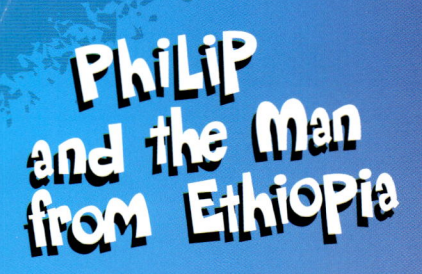

Acts 8:26-40

This is Philip, one of the apostles. Philip preached the good news of Jesus in many places. One day an angel of the Lord spoke to Philip and said, "Go south to the desert road." So Philip started out, and he met an important Ethiopian official. The official had gone to Jerusalem to worship, and he was now returning home. He was sitting in his chariot reading the book of Isaiah.

The Holy Spirit said to Philip, "Go to that chariot."

Philip ran over and asked, "Do you understand what you are reading?"

The man replied, "How can I? I need someone to explain it to me. Can you tell me who the prophet is talking about?"

So beginning with this Scripture in Isaiah, Philip told the man the good news about Jesus. As they rode along, they came to some water and the man said, "Look! Here is water! What can stop me from being baptized?"

So Philip and the official went down into the water, and Philip baptized him.

When they came up out of the water, the Spirit of the Lord suddenly took Philip away to another town. The Ethiopian official never saw Philip again but went on his way, full of joy.

Saul Becomes a Believer

Acts 9:1-31

This is Saul. Saul was a Pharisee who hated the followers of Jesus so much that he would arrest them and take them to Jerusalem so they could be put to death.

Saul was on his way to Damascus to arrest more followers when suddenly a light from heaven flashed around him. He fell to the ground and heard a voice say, "Saul! Saul! Why are you opposing me?"

Saul asked, "Who are you, Lord?"

And the voice said, "I am Jesus. Now get up and go into the city. There you will be told what you must do."

Saul got up and he opened his eyes, but he couldn't see anything. So the men who were with Saul led him into the city.

After three days, God sent Ananias, a follower of Jesus, to go to Saul. Ananias put his hands on Saul, and right away something like scales fell from Saul's eyes and he could see again. Saul became a follower of Jesus and was baptized.

Saul began teaching people that Jesus is the Son of God. All who heard him were amazed that the man who wanted to arrest the followers of Jesus was proving that Jesus is the Messiah.

Saul started to go by a new name—Paul.

He traveled to many places, preaching to all people. Despite many hard times like being imprisoned, shipwrecked, and narrowly escaping death, Paul continued to do everything he could to save people and help them know God. And many came to know Jesus because of what Paul said. Paul taught many through letters that he wrote to groups of believers. Because of Paul's letters, even more people have come to learn about Jesus, and his letters can be read in the Bible even to this day.

Paul and Silas in Prison

Acts 16:16-40

One day Paul was going to pray with his friend Silas. On the way, they were followed by a girl who was controlled by an evil spirit that helped her tell people what was going to happen. Her owners used her to make money.

Paul told the evil spirit, "In the name of Jesus Christ, I command you to come out of her!" At that very moment, the girl was freed.

But her owners got mad at Paul and Silas because they couldn't make any more money from her predictions. They dragged them to the town's authorities, who ordered Paul and Silas to be beaten and thrown in prison.

The jailer locked them up deep in the prison to make sure they wouldn't escape. Around midnight, Paul and Silas were praying and singing to God. The other prisoners were listening.

Suddenly, there was a powerful earthquake. The prison doors flew open, and the chains of all the prisoners fell off. But Paul and Silas didn't leave even though they could have.

Several people decided to follow Jesus that night, including the jailer and his whole family.

The next morning, Paul and Silas were released from jail and the city authorities even apologized to them. Paul and Silas encouraged the followers of Jesus in the town to be brave and then continued on their way to tell more people about Jesus.

Not the End

John 20:31; Romans 10:9-10; Ephesians 2:10; 3:20; Revelation 11:15; 21:1-5; 22:1-5

The Bible begins in the garden with Adam and Eve. They disobeyed God, and the world was never the same. Sin entered the world, and we couldn't be with our perfect God anymore. But God still loved Adam and Eve, and he had a plan to bring everyone into his family. That plan was Jesus.

Jesus came and lived a perfect life on earth. Jesus is the Son of God and the Savior of the world. All these stories are written so that you may believe that Jesus is the Messiah, the Son of God.

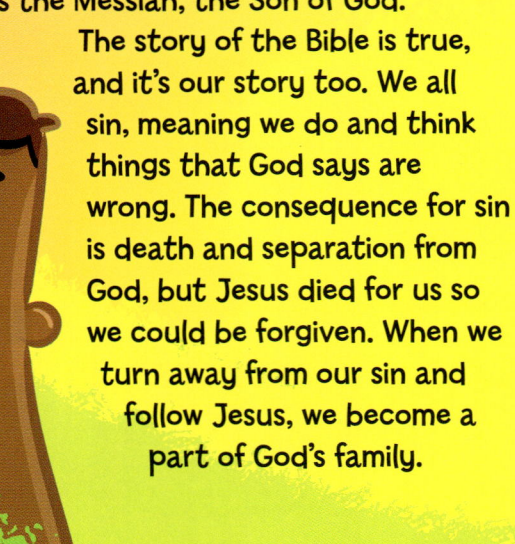

The story of the Bible is true, and it's our story too. We all sin, meaning we do and think things that God says are wrong. The consequence for sin is death and separation from God, but Jesus died for us so we could be forgiven. When we turn away from our sin and follow Jesus, we become a part of God's family.

If you want to make the choice to follow Jesus, you can pray this prayer to him, or talk to God about it in your own way!

God, thank you for loving me and saving me. I believe your Son, Jesus, came to die for my sins. I know I have sinned and done things that are wrong, but I want you to be in my life. Please forgive me. I love you! Amen.

The Bible says when we believe in our hearts and say with our mouths that Jesus is Lord, we are saved. Now you get to go on an incredible journey with Jesus! You are God's masterpiece, and he has created you to do good things that he planned for you long ago. He has a purpose and plan for you. With his power working in you, God is able to do far more than you could ever ask for or imagine.

This is not the end. God's story isn't over. Jesus is coming back. God will take everything that is broken and make it new. There will be no tears, no death, no sadness, and no pain. We will see God's face, and we will live with him. For we are his people and his children.

The Lord will rule forever and ever. Amen!

Hey-O!